Family and Professional Guardianship

A COMPLETE PLANNING GUIDE
Guardianship of Adults
and Children
with Dementia, Alzheimer's, and
Developmental Disabilities

Family and Professional Guardianship

A COMPLETE PLANNING GUIDE
Guardianship of Adults
and Children
with Dementia, Alzheimer's, and
Developmental Disabilities

Homer L. Hartage

Copyright ©2024 by The Hartage Foundation
First Edition 2024
All Rights Reserved
Written by Homer L. Hartage
Published by The Hartage Foundation Inc.
PO Box 560245
Orlando, Florida 32856
homer.hartage@agedcareguardian.com

Library of Congress Control Number: 2024902777

ISBN: 979-8-98880443-0-6 Hardback
ISBN: 979-8-9888044-1-3 Paperback

No part of this book may be photocopied, reproduced, distributed electronically or otherwise, stored in any retrieval system, or transmitted in any way without the prior written permission of the publisher.

Legal Disclaimer

While the author and all associated contributors have made every effort to present accurate and up to date information within this document, it is apparent that laws, technologies, and information rapidly change. Therefore, the author and all associated contributors reserve the right to update the contents and information provided herein as these changes progress. The author and/or all associated contributors take no responsibility for any errors or omissions if such discrepancies exist within this document.

The author and all other contributors accept no responsibility for any consequential actions taken, whether monetary, legal, or otherwise, by any and all readers of the materials provided. It is the readers sole responsibility to seek professional advice before taking any action on their part.

Readers' results will vary based on their skill level and individual perception of the contents herein, and thus no guarantees, monetarily or otherwise, can be made accurately. Therefore, no guarantees are made by the authors or associated contributors.

Dedication

This book is dedicated to all the past and present clients of AgedCare, who inspire me daily, and to my late mother, Leverna, who instilled in me a spirit of caring for others and a passion for life-long learning. Mama, it worked.

Epigraph

We never know how good we are until we are called to rise.
— Emily Dickinson

Table of Contents

Table of Contents xi

1. Introduction 1

   Why Do We Need a Book on Guardianship in Florida 1

   1.1. What is Guardianship 5

   1.2 Types of Guardianship 6

   1.3. Guardianship in Florida 9

   1.3.1. Overview 9

   1.3.2. Legal Criteria for Appointing a Guardian in Florida 11

   1.3.3. The Guardianship Process in Florida 12

   1.4. The Hartage Foundation Inc. dba AgedCare 14

   1.4.1. History of AgedCare 14

1.4.2. Mission Statement 15
1.4.3. Company Summary 15
1.4.4. Why Guardians Need an Exit Plan... 17
2. The History of Guardianship...................... 19
2.1. Overview 19
2.2. Roman Law and English Common Law: Roman Law – The Origins of Western Guardianship 21
3. The Guardianship Appointment Process: Steps and Requirements........ 23
3.1. Overview 23
3.2. Who Can Become a Guardian........... 24
3.3. The Path Towards Guardianship 28
3.3.1. Determining Incapacity 28
3.3.1.1. Criteria for Determining Incapacity...................................... 29
3.3.1.2. Assessment by the Examining Committee 34
3.3.1.3 Appealing a Determination of Incapacity...................................... 41
3.3.2. Filing a Petition for Guardianship 57

3.3.2.1. Notice Requirements 57

3.3.2.2. Filing Fees 63

3.3.2.3. Preparing the Petition................. 67

3.3.2.4. Finding a Representing Attorney 71

3.4. Chapter Summary 73

4. Guardian Compensation in Florida........... 79

   4.1. Overview... 79

   4.2. Professional Guardians 82

   4.2.1. Compensation Options.................. 82

4.2.1.1. Hourly and Flat Fee Compensation for Professional Guardians..................................... 83

4.2.1.2. Reimbursement for Expenses for Professional Guardians..................................... 85

4.2.1.3. Allowances and Stipends for Professional Guardians.................. 87

4.2.2. Determination and Approval of Professional Guardian Compensation 87

   4.3. Family Guardians 88

   4.3.1. Compensation Options.................. 88

4.3.1.1. Hourly and Flat Fee Compensation for Family Guardians 89

4.3.1.2. Reimbursement for Expenses for Family Guardians 91

4.3.1.3. Miscellaneous Compensation for Family Guardians 92

4.3.2. Determination and Approval of Compensation for Family Guardians 93

4.4. Differences Between Compensation for Professional and Family Guardians in Florida 93

4.5. Source of Compensation for Professional and Family Guardians 95

4.6. Challenges and Ethical Considerations Associated with Guardian Compensation 97

4.7. Chapter Summary 100

5. Governing Body & Guardianship Reporting in Florida 103

5.1. Overview 103

Case Study - Ms. Bee 105

5.2. Governing Body 110

5.2.1. Department of Elder Affairs......... 110

5.2.2. Clerk of Court 111

5.2.3. Circuit Court 112

5.3. Guardianship Reporting in Florida 113

5.3.1. Reports – Plan and Inventory 113

5.3.2 Understanding Reporting periods 122

5.3.3. Record Keeping and Case Notes... 125

5.4. Chapter Summary 126

6. Determining When Guardianship is Needed... 129

6.1. Overview....................................... 129

6.2. Guardianship for Persons with Substance Abuse and Other Mental Disorders........................ 132

6.2.2. Marchman Act 140

6.3. Alternatives to Guardianship 149

6.3.1. Durable Power of Attorney........... 149

6.3.2. Designation of Heath Care Surrogate 156

6.4. Chapter Summary............................ 161
7. Placement of Incapacitated Persons and Costs.. 165
   7.1. Overview 165
   7.2. Home or Community Placement 171
   7.3. Independent Living.......................... 175
   7.4. Assisted Living Facility (ALF).......... 178
   7.5. Nursing Home.................................. 180
   7.6. Skilled Nursing Facility 182
   7.7. Using Professional Placement Services... 184
   7.8. Costs of Placement of Incapacitated Persons in Florida... 191
   7.9. Chapter Summary............................ 193
8. Funding for Care and Placement............. 195
   8.1. Overview 195
   8.2. Retirement Benefits......................... 200
   8.3. Medicaid 205
   8.4. Medicare 215
   8.5. Railroad Retirement Benefits........... 218
   8.6. Social Security Benefits................... 221

8.6.1. Retirement Benefits 221

8.6.2. Survivor Benefits 223

8.6.3. Disability Benefits (SSDI) 224

8.6.4. The Supplemental Security Income (SSI) 225

8.6.5. Other programs 226

8.7. Private Programs 229

8.7.1. Insurance 229

8.7.2. Annuities 231

8.7.3. Individual Retirement Account (IRA) 232

8.7.4. Mutual Funds 233

8.7.5. Bank accounts 235

8.7.6. Assets 235

8.8. Chapter Summary 236

9. Managing Guardianship 239

9.1. Overview 239

Case Study – Lynn's Story 241

9.2. Getting a Guardian 246

9.3. Resigning and Removing a Guardian 250

9.3.1. Resigning a Guardian 250

- 9.3.2. Removing A Guardian 252
- 9.4 How to File a Complaint in Florida... 255
  - 9.4.1. Florida Office of Public and Professional Guardians (OPPG).... 255
  - 9.4.2. Clerk of the Court 256
  - 9.4.3. Judicial Qualifications Commission 257
- 9.5. Chapter Summary.......................... 259
- 10. Conclusion and Summary 263
  - 10.1 Modern Day & The Future of Guardianship 263
  - 10.2 What's Broken in Florida's Guardian System and How Can We Fix It?............................ 273
  - 10.3 What is the Future of Guardianship? 275
- GLOSSARY 279
- Appendix 1 283
- Appendix 2 291
- Bibliographies By Chapter 299
  - Chapter 1 299
  - Chapter 2 300

Chapter 3 304

Chapter 4 305

Chapter 5 306

Chapter 6 308

Chapter 7 310

Chapter 8 311

Chapter 9 313

1. Introduction

Why Do We Need a Book on Guardianship in Florida

Let's face it. In addition to the emotional turmoil that goes along with seeking and obtaining guardianship, families are often confused and overwhelmed by the legal process. I have known for some time that there was a need for a more definitive book on this process in Florida, a book that would help explain in more simple terms how it all works, what options are available, what to do, and what to expect.

There are an increasing number of elderly and otherwise incapacitated individuals who feel alone, overwhelmed. Where can they turn for help? Millions have the same concerns.

One guardianship case drove this point home for me more than any other. It made me keenly aware of the meaningful benefits of closely listening to clients under guardianship, even when diagnosed with dementia or other disabilities.

The story starts in September 2022, when I met a female *ward*, as they are called in Florida. I'll call her Lynn.

I was assigned as Lynn's guardian in July of 2022 and was the successor of two previous guardians. Lynn's case was thought by the courts and by me (initially) to be an indigent guardianship case. This assumption is what brought us together, as my office would regularly take pro bono cases. It turned out that Lynn wasn't indigent at all. There was no financial reason for her to live in the conditions I found her - poor, alone, with limited access to the comforts of the life she had been accustomed to. Lynn's net worth was nearly four hundred thousand dollars (more on this later).

Is Lynn's case unique, or does it reflect the presence of barriers to quality service provided to incapacitated persons in Florida? Lynn's case is not unique. There are barriers, and this is something we'll explore in this book. A search of Google and Amazon will leave you wondering why more has not been done to provide families and care professionals with at least some basic information on guardianship.

Introduction

There are, however, a few books on the subject. One such book is *The Fundamentals of Guardianship*, published by the National Guardianship Association. This book contains a lot of helpful information on guardianship, but it is mainly directed at guardianship professionals. Its subtitle *What Every Guardian Should Know* says it all. Furthermore, it is a general textbook and does not address the unique needs of Florida guardianships.

There are several books that do address the Florida guardianship program. While these works advance our understanding of guardianship, most of them are outdated. There is one book, however, *Florida Guardianship: Who Shall Live and Who Should Die*, by Beverly Rochelle Newman that does address what families need to make clear decisions on selecting a guardian.

To fill this gap, I will address this topic in simple but informative ways. Throughout the book, readers will learn how Florida guardianship works. I will begin by explaining what guardianship is and its specific application in Florida, as well as introducing AgedCare, a resource of The Hartage Foundation Inc., a nonprofit organization that supports professional guardianship and scholarship.

Next, I will explain the different types of guardianship, including person, property, limited, voluntary, guardian advocate, veteran, plenary, family, and professional guardianship. We will then delve into the appointment process for becoming a guardian, including who can become a guardian, the steps and requirements for obtaining guardianship, and the role of the examining committee.

One chapter will be dedicated to discussing the topic of guardian compensation in Florida, including the differences between professional and family guardians. In addition, I will examine the governing body and guardianship reporting requirements in Florida, including the Department of Elder Affairs, Clerk of Court, the Probate Circuit Court, and the various reporting periods and documents required.

I will also provide an evidence-based perspective on when guardianship is needed, including for persons with substance abuse and other mental disorders, as well as alternatives to guardianship such as durable power of attorney and health care surrogate designation. The placement options for incapacitated persons and the associated costs will also be addressed, as will the funding options for care and placement, such as retirement benefits, Medicaid, Medicare, and veterans' benefits.

You will also learn about the management of guardianship, including getting, resigning, and removing a guardian, as well as discharging a guardian and filing a complaint in Florida.

I will share case studies and actual field examples to help readers gain helpful insight that will address your needs for a guardian for your loved one. You will read about success stories, difficult cases, problems and occasional errors made, and how I was able to address them.

The ultimate goal of this book is to serve as a guide that will make nearly any guardian case succeed.

1.1. What is Guardianship

Guardianship is a legal process in which a court appoints an individual or entity to make decisions on behalf of another person who is deemed incapacitated and unable to make decisions for themselves. The purpose of guardianship is to protect the well-being and interests of the incapacitated person, also known as the *ward*, by ensuring that they receive proper care and protection.

The legal definition of guardianship can vary by jurisdiction, but it generally refers to the authority and responsibility of a guardian to make decisions and act on behalf of a ward in accordance with the law. Guardianship can be granted over an individual's person, property, or both. It can be used to make decisions related to the ward's personal care, safety and well-being, medical treatment, residence and living arrangements, education, and financial management.

As a general rule, guardianship is a measure of last resort and is typically used when other less restrictive alternatives, such as the power of attorney or a healthcare surrogate, are not appropriate or available.

But guardians are also responsible for protecting their ward's assets and property and must keep accurate records of the ward's financial and personal information. They must report to the court on a regular basis about the ward's condition and the actions taken on their behalf.

1.2 Types of Guardianship

There are several types of guardianship.

1. *Person guardianship* is used to make decisions about the ward's personal care and well-being. This includes decisions about medical treatment, living arrangements, and personal relationships.

2. *Property guardianship* is used to manage the ward's financial and property affairs. This includes decisions about the ward's assets, income, and expenses.
3. *Limited guardianship* is a type of guardianship that is used when the ward only needs assistance in specific areas of their life, such as managing their finances or making decisions about their medical care.
4. *Voluntary guardianship* is when a person voluntarily gives up the power to make decisions about their own personal care and well-being and gives it to another person.
5. *Guardian advocate* is a type of guardianship that is used for individuals with developmental disabilities. This type of guardianship allows the guardian to make decisions about the ward's personal care and well-being, as well as decisions about their education and training.
6. *Veteran guardianship* is applied to veterans who are unable to make decisions about their own personal care and well-being due to a disability related to their military service.
7. *Plenary guardianship* is a type of guardianship that gives the guardian complete control over the ward's personal care and well-being, as well as their financial and property affairs.

8. *Family guardianship* is appointed to a family member of the ward
9. *Professional guardianship* is a type of guardianship that is appointed to a professional guardian who is responsible for the ward's personal care and well-being, as well as their financial and property affairs.

Each type of guardianship has its own unique purpose and responsibilities, and it is important to understand the differences between them in order to make informed decisions about the care and well-being of the ward.

The process of determining incapacity is often initiated by a family member, friend, or healthcare professional who has concerns about the individual's ability to make decisions. This is where many families and loved ones find the process distasteful. Guilt and shame may cloud their decision, but this must be thought through logically and with as little emotion as possible to determine what is in the best interest of the ward.

Once the petition for guardianship is filed, the court will appoint a neutral third party, such as a physician, to evaluate the individual and determine if they meet the legal criteria for incapacity. The criteria for incapacity vary by state but generally include the inability to understand the nature and consequences of decisions, the inability to communicate decisions, and or the inability to meet basic needs.

Once the court determines that the individual is incapacitated, they will appoint a guardian to make decisions on their behalf. The legal criteria for appointing a guardian include the ward's preference, the suitability of the proposed guardian, and the least restrictive option for the ward. The relationship between guardianship and incapacity is rooted in the principle of protecting the ward's best interests, while also ensuring their autonomy and rights are respected to the greatest extent possible.

1.3. Guardianship in Florida

1.3.1. Overview

In the state of Florida, guardianship is a legal process in which a court appoints an individual or entity to make decisions on behalf of another person who is deemed incapacitated. Guardianship in Florida can be divided into two types: *guardianship of the person*, which deals with the ward's personal needs, and *guardianship of the property*, which deals with the ward's financial and property matters.

The Florida guardianship process begins with a petition for guardianship filed by an interested party, such as a family member or friend, in the circuit court of the county where the ward resides. The court will then hold a hearing to determine the ward's incapacity and whether the appointment of a guardian is necessary. If the court finds that the ward is incapacitated, it will appoint a guardian and set out the scope of the guardian's powers and responsibilities.

In Florida, guardianship is overseen by the Office of Public and Professional Guardians, which is responsible for ensuring that guardians are qualified, trained, and fulfilling their responsibilities in accordance with the law. The office also investigates complaints against guardians and can take action to remove a guardian if necessary.

As in other states, problems with public guardianship range from the quantity and quality of unfulfilled demand for services to negative outcomes for guardianship and other protective services. The absence of decision-making capacity and a legal guardian result in extended hospital stays for critically ill patients in ICU, with a median length twice as long compared to other ICU patients.

The first national study on public guardianship evaluated how it affects the ability of individuals with legal incapacity to access their rights, benefits, and entitlements. The study revealed a requirement for public guardianship and some cases of effective advocacy, but also uncovered issues such as understaffing, underfunding, and overburdening of public guardian offices, neglect of many individuals under public guardianship, and instances of abuse.

A more recent national study showed that nearly all public guardianship programs suffer from insufficient staffing and funding, undertrained and underpaid staff, limited and poorly managed data systems, and a lack of protections against improper coercion in due process.

1.3.2. Legal Criteria for Appointing a Guardian in Florida

In the state of Florida, a guardian can be appointed by the court for a person who has been determined to be incapacitated. Incapacity is defined as a condition in which a person is unable to manage their property or make decisions about their own welfare due to a physical or mental impairment. The legal criteria for appointing a guardian in Florida are outlined in the Florida Statutes, Section 744.

According to the statute, a person can be found incapacitated if they are unable to perform at least one of the following tasks without assistance:

- Provide their own food, clothing, or shelter
- Attend to their own physical health
- Manage their own financial affairs
- Understand the nature and consequences of their decisions

Additionally, the statute states that in order for a guardian to be appointed, there must be clear and convincing evidence that the person is incapacitated. This evidence can come from a medical examination, psychiatric evaluation, or other relevant information. The court will also consider any alternatives to guardianship, such as a power of attorney or a trust, before appointing a guardian.

1.3.3. The Guardianship Process in Florida

The guardianship process in Florida is established by state law and is governed by the Florida

Probate Code. The process begins with the filing of a petition for guardianship in the appropriate circuit court. The petition must include specific information about the proposed ward, including their current living situation and medical condition.

Once the petition is filed, the court will appoint *guardian ad litem* (GAL) to investigate and report to the court on the proposed ward's needs and whether guardianship is necessary. The GAL will also investigate any potential conflicts of interest between the proposed ward and the proposed guardian.

The court will also set a hearing date for the petition, and notice of the hearing must be provided to the proposed ward, their relatives, and any interested parties. The ward has the right to be represented by an attorney at the hearing.

After the hearing, the court will make a determination on whether to appoint a guardian. If the court finds that a guardian is necessary, it will also determine the type of guardianship that is appropriate, such as a guardianship of the person, the property, or both.

Once a guardian is appointed, they are required to file regular reports with the court and must follow all court-ordered conditions of the guardianship. The ward also has the right to request a review of the guardianship at any time, and the court can also initiate a review on its own motion.

In Florida, the Uniform Guardianship and Protective Proceedings Act (UGPPA) outlines the rights and procedures for adults who are unable to make decisions regarding their person or property and need a guardian to assist them. The UGPPA provides a framework for the court to follow when determining whether guardianship is necessary and what type of guardianship is appropriate.

1.4. The Hartage Foundation Inc. dba AgedCare

1.4.1. History of AgedCare

Inspired by a visit to The Florida Frist Firm, a group of medical and elder law attorneys, I envisioned a similar agency model for my guardianship business. This office, with its team of attorneys and 12 or so employees, was successfully fulfilling its social service mission. I realized that this approach could work for a guardianship office, as currently nearly all guardianship offices in Florida are solo practices, with only one or two staff members.

To bring this vision to life, I used an established Foundation, the Hartage Foundation Inc. which was founded in 2007 as a non-profit 501(c)3 organization. Under the foundation, I launched AgedCare in 2017 as a Professional Guardianship Company. This company has a fully staffed office, including a case manager, property and asset manager, an office marketing manager, and a guardian.

1.4.2. Mission Statement

The mission of the Hartage Foundation Inc., d/b/a AgedCare, is to care and to serve, to be an industry leading guardianship company that provides advocacy and support to persons in need who, due to incapacity, lack the ability to manage their affairs.

We believe that this mission statement is important because it guides our actions and decisions, and helps us stay focused on our ultimate goal of providing the highest level of care and service to our clients.

1.4.3. Company Summary

The Nonprofit Corporate Guardianship model, as it is called in Florida, offers long-term stability for the wards, the guardian, and any potential successor guardian. With this model, the guardianship business can be transferred as a whole, rather than in parts, as is currently done when a guardian is removed, resigns, or retires. The Hartage Foundation, Inc. acts as the guardian, which is a significant distinction in the guardianship process.

This stability and continuity can be achieved through the use of automation and a dedicated staff. AgedCare, the professional guardianship company established by the Hartage Foundation, currently employs six full-time staff members, including an office manager, a property and asset manager, two guardians, two case managers, and a companion care staff member. These employees allow the office to expand services to clients, delegate responsibilities, improve oversight, maintain timely reporting, and consolidate client file documents. All of these elements are crucial for a well-designed transition plan in the event of the death, disability, or retirement of the guardian.

Furthermore, state regulations require all employees to be approved by the Department of Elder Affairs, which includes a Level 2 background check and a credit check. Automation also plays a vital role in the process by allowing for the centralization of client information and creating a transparent operation.

The Hartage Foundation provides professional guardianship services throughout the state of Florida, with initial operations in Orange, Lake, Seminole, Volusia, and Osceola Counties.

1.4.4. Why Guardians Need an Exit Plan

The corporate guardianship model, also known as the nonprofit model, offers a solution to the issue of guardianship succession. It is important for a business plan to include an orderly process for the guardian to retire while ensuring consistent care for the wards under their supervision.

This is not only fair to the clients, but it also eliminates the uncertainty and chaos currently present in the system. It is not just to leave the fate of the wards solely in the hands of the courts without a comprehensive file and client history for a successor guardian to reference. A properly designed and executed transition plan, with the help of automation and staff, can provide a smooth transition for both the ward and the successor guardian.

At The National Guardianship Association Conference a few years ago, I spoke with a fellow guardian about operating a business in this field. She looked at me with disapproval and said, "You're just in it for the money." As a new guardian, this comment was hurtful. Like so many, I entered this profession to serve and support others. This is paramount and the foundation of guardianship.

But as I thought more on her comment, things became clearer. If you are in this business solely for the money, then this is the wrong field for you. On the other hand, being a good businessperson is equally important to ensure the success and well-being of our wards.

With the advent of the COVID-19 pandemic and the realization of how quickly things can change, it has become imperative for guardians to have a plan in place for transitioning their business. Ignoring this issue is no longer an option.

There are various models for guardianship business operations across the country and they operate under different names; for example, they are called guardians in Florida and conservators in Connecticut.

2. The History of Guardianship

2.1. Overview

While this book is focused on Florida guardianship programs, it is helpful to look at key moments in the history of guardianship. This is not intended to be a complete history, but an overview on key historical movements that have influenced guardianship in Florida. This brief review allows us to clearly see the roots of Florida guardianship law and how closely it aligns with the historical views and application of guardianship.

Since the beginning of recorded history, guardianship of minors and the infirmed has been part of the civil law. Our forefathers and foremothers understood the value of guardianship. They valued the need to protect the property of those unable to do so themselves. They knew that protecting orphan minors and securing the health, safety and security of persons living in the margins of the population due to illness, incapacity, disability – including socio-economic depravity – was in the best interest of society.

Scholars generally believe that modern guardianship is based on the Roman Law of Guardianship. Then, too, guardians were appointed to care for and protect minors, individuals with mental disabilities, and other individuals who were unable to care for themselves. I was, in fact, struck by how many similarities exist between Florida guardianship regulations and the historical Roman Law of Guardianship.

Like today, laws regulating guardianship in ancient Rome dealt with the various types of guardianship, to whom guardianship would have applied, compensation, petitions and application for guardianship, reporting, and dealing with exportation.

Florida's guardianship system has also been influenced by the English Common Law, itself strongly influenced by the Roman law, and by several other historical events – including the Spanish era and various legal developments in the United States as a whole.

Given that Western guardianship appears to have its roots in Ancient Rome, it seems appropriate to start the review with a few paragraphs on guardianship under the Roman law.

2.2. Roman Law and English Common Law: Roman Law – The Origins of Western Guardianship

According to the work of legal scholar John Witte Jr. (2007), Roman law recognized the concept of *tutela*, which designated a guardian to manage the legal and financial affairs of an individual deemed unable to do so, such as a minor or incapacitated adult. This system was based on the idea that the state had a responsibility to protect those who were unable to protect themselves. The "tutor" or guardian was appointed by the state and had the authority to make decisions on behalf of the *tutee* or ward, including marriage, property transactions, and legal matters.

In Roman law, there were two types of guardianship, *tutela* for minors and *cura* for the insane. Tutela for minors was automatically terminated at the age of 14 for males and 12 for females, and cura for the insane ended when the person was restored to sanity. Roman law also recognized the right of parents to act as guardians for their children.

Roman law also incorporated the concept of *boni viri* or "good men" who could be appointed as guardians. These were individuals who were deemed morally upright and capable of fulfilling the responsibilities of a guardian. This concept laid the foundation for the idea of a neutral third-party guardian, who could act in the best interests of the ward, rather than the guardian being appointed by the state or the ward's family.

The place of Roman law in the history of English law has long been a subject of interest and debate. At least since the seventeenth century, scholars have scrutinized the pages and procedures of ancient texts, as well as the acts of Parliament to detect possible civilian influence.

The results have not been conclusive. In the end, the question remains open: What influence, if any, has Roman law had on the course of English legal development?

3. The Guardianship Appointment Process: Steps and Requirements

3.1. Overview

Guardianship appointment can be a complex and confusing process. In the state of Florida, the guardianship appointment process involves several steps, including someone filing a petition for guardianship, the appointment of examining committees, a determination of incapacity, and court hearings.

Whether you are considering becoming a guardian or seeking guardianship for someone close to you, you should have a strong understanding of the requirements and processes involved in the appointment process.

The goal of this chapter is to assist readers in navigating through the complex process of guardianship appointments. To achieve this goal, I will present a detailed account of each step involved in guardianship appointments along with additional relevant information.

This chapter will cover everything from who can become a guardian to the specific documents and forms that must be filed with the court to initiate the guardianship process. I will also discuss the criteria that are used to determine incapacity, which is often a key factor in the appointment of a guardian.

Unfortunately, vulnerable individuals are often targeted by those who seek to take advantage of them by exploiting their vulnerabilities for personal gain.

Understanding the guardianship appointment process can help you protect yourself and those close to you against abuses and ensure that vulnerable individuals get the best care possible.

3.2. Who Can Become a Guardian

A guardian is a person who is appointed by a court to act as a legal representative for another person who is unable to make important

3. Appointment Process: Steps and Requirements

decisions for themselves. The person who needs a guardian is usually a minor or an adult with a disability or impairment that makes them unable to care for themselves or manage their own affairs.

The role of a guardian can vary depending on the specific needs and circumstances of the person they are appointed to represent. In general, a guardian has the legal authority to make decisions on behalf of the person they are representing, including decisions about medical care, living arrangements, financial matters, and other important issues.

In the state of Florida, the process of appointing a guardian involves a detailed court process. There are specific requirements that must be met in order to be eligible for an appointment as a guardian.

- **Age Requirement.** In Florida, the age requirement for becoming a guardian is 18 years old or older. This means that in order to act as a guardian the potential guardian must be at least 18 years old.
- **Residency Requirement.** The potential guardian must be a resident of the state of Florida, unless the individual in need of a

guardian is not a Florida resident, but has property located in the state of Florida.

- **Criminal Background Check Requirement.** Potential guardians are required to undergo a level 2, criminal background check in order to be appointed as a guardian. The criminal background check is designed to ensure that the potential guardian does not have a history of criminal activity that would make them ineligible for the role.

- **Disqualifying Factors.** There are certain disqualifying factors that can prevent someone from being appointed as a guardian in Florida. These disqualifying factors include:

    1. A history of abuse, neglect, or exploitation of elderly or disabled individuals.
    2. A history of any felony convictions, including fraud, embezzlement, or financial exploitation.
    3. A history of chronic alcohol or drug abuse
    4. A conflict of interest, such as a financial interest in the individual's estate.

3. Appointment Process: Steps and Requirements

5. Any other factor that would make the individual unsuitable to act as a guardian.
6. Poor credit history.

- **Other Considerations.** In addition to meeting the requirements and avoiding disqualifying factors, there are other considerations that may be important when deciding whether to become a guardian in Florida. These may include:

    1. Time commitment: Acting as a guardian can require a significant time commitment, and it is important to consider whether you have the time and resources to fulfill this role.
    2. Emotional involvement: Acting as a guardian can also be emotionally challenging, particularly if the person in need of a guardian is a close family member or friend. It is important to consider whether you can maintain objectivity and make decisions in the best interests of the person you are representing.
    3. Financial responsibility: Depending on the type of guardianship role, you may be responsible for managing the

financial affairs of the person in need of a guardian. You may want to consider whether you have the financial knowledge and responsibility to fulfill this role.
4. Legal responsibility: As a guardian, you will have legal responsibility for the person you are representing. It is essential to be aware of the legal requirements and procedures that must be followed.

3.3. The Path Towards Guardianship

The path toward guardianship in Florida involves a detailed court process, which is designed to ensure that the individual in need of a guardian receives appropriate care and protection.

3.3.1. Determining Incapacity

Determining incapacity is an important step in the process of appointing a guardian. Incapacity is a legal determination that means the individual is unable to make important decisions for themselves in certain areas, such as decisions related to medical care, living arrangements, and financial matters.

3. Appointment Process: Steps and Requirements

In Florida, the determination of incapacity is made by a court-appointed examining committee, which is made up of at least three members, including a physician and two other professionals with experience working with individuals who have disabilities or impairments.

The Examining Committee will evaluate the individual's medical condition, mental status, and ability to make decisions, and will submit a report to the court with their findings. If the examining committee determines that the individual is incapacitated in all or some areas, the court will move forward with the guardianship appointment process.

3.3.1.1. Criteria for Determining Incapacity

Determining incapacity is a critical step in the process of appointing a guardian in the state of Florida. It is a legal process that involves assessing an individual's ability to make decisions and care for themselves. The determination must be based on clear and convincing evidence, which means that the evidence must be highly persuasive and leave no doubt in the court's mind.

The criteria for determining incapacity in Florida are set forth in Chapter 744 of the Florida Statutes and include:

- Assessing an individual's ability to understand and appreciate consequences.
- Their ability to manage their own affairs.
- The presence of a "mental or physical condition that prevents them from exercising reasonable judgment in the conduct of their affairs."

Specifically, the statute provides that an individual may be considered incapacitated if they have a mental illness, developmental disability, organic brain damage, or other mental or physical impairment that results in the individual being unable to make informed decisions. In addition, expert evaluation and other relevant factors may be considered in the determination of incapacity.

When assessing the individual's ability to manage their own affairs, the court may consider several factors, such as their ability to feed, bathe, and dress themselves, their ability to manage their medication, and their ability to maintain their living environment. The court may also assess the individual's ability to manage their financial affairs, such as paying bills and managing their budget.

For example, an individual who is unable to manage their financial affairs may be unable to pay their rent or utility bills, which could lead to

3. Appointment Process: Steps and Requirements

eviction or disconnection of services. Similarly, an individual who is unable to manage their medication may fail to take their medication correctly, which could lead to serious health complications.

When an individual is unable to manage their affairs, it may be necessary to appoint a guardian to assist them with specific tasks or decision-making. The type of guardianship will depend on the level of assistance required, and the court may appoint a guardian of the person, a guardian of the property, or a limited guardian, depending on the individual's needs.

The court will also consider the presence of mental or physical incapacity when determining incapacity. Mental incapacity may include conditions such as dementia, Alzheimer's disease, or other cognitive impairments that may affect an individual's decision-making ability. Physical incapacity may include conditions such as paralysis, blindness, or other physical limitations that may impact an individual's ability to care for themselves.

When assessing the presence of mental or physical incapacity, the court will evaluate the individual's medical and mental health status. This may include medical records, psychiatric evaluations, or other documentation that can provide insight into the individual's condition.

For example, an individual who has been diagnosed with advanced Alzheimer's disease may be unable to make informed decisions, manage their medication, or perform activities of daily living. Similarly, an individual who has suffered a traumatic brain injury may experience cognitive impairments that impact their ability to understand and appreciate consequences or manage their affairs.

The presence of mental or physical incapacity may lead to the appointment of a guardian to assist the individual with decision-making and care. The court will evaluate the level of assistance required and may appoint a guardian of the person, a guardian of the property, or a limited guardian, depending on the results of the evaluation.

The court may also rely on expert evaluation as a criterion to assess an individual's ability to care for themselves. An expert evaluation may be conducted by a mental health professional, physician, or another qualified specialist who can provide insight into the individual's medical and mental health status.

3. Appointment Process: Steps and Requirements

The expert evaluation can include a comprehensive assessment of the individual's cognitive functioning, emotional and behavioral functioning, and physical abilities. The evaluation can also include a review of the individual's medical records, medication history, and other relevant information.

For example, an expert evaluation may be conducted on an individual who has been diagnosed with dementia to assess their ability to understand and appreciate consequences, manage their own affairs, and care for themselves. The evaluation may include cognitive testing, assessments of their activities of daily living, and a review of their medical history.

The results of the expert evaluation are considered valid evidence to support the court's determination of incapacity. The expert's recommendations may also be considered when appointing a guardian to assist the individual with decision-making and care.

The court may provide guidance on the qualifications required for expert evaluations and may require the expert to provide a written report that outlines their findings and recommendations.

There are several other factors that the court may consider when making a determination.

These factors can be unique to the individual and impact their ability to care for themselves.

Examples include substance abuse, physical limitations, or medication side effects that can affect an individual's decision-making capacity or ability to manage their own affairs. The court also considers the individual's wishes, if known, and the opinions of their family members, caregivers, or other individuals involved in their care.

The court needs to evaluate all relevant factors and use clear and convincing evidence to make a determination of incapacity.

It is important to consider an individual's unique circumstances when assessing their capacity to care for themselves. The court needs to make use of as much relevant information as possible to make an informed decision.

3.3.1.2. Assessment by the Examining Committee

When an individual's capacity to care for themselves is called into question, a court may order an evaluation by the Examining Committee to determine the individual's mental and physical condition.

3. Appointment Process: Steps and Requirements

In Florida, the Examining Committee is typically composed of three members: a physician, a psychiatrist or psychologist, and a layperson. The committee's purpose is to evaluate the individual's mental and physical condition and provide a report to the court detailing their findings.

The committee will interview the individual and may also speak with family members, caregivers, and other individuals who have knowledge of the individual's condition. The committee may also review medical records, financial statements, and other relevant documents.

The examination process is an essential step. Its purpose is to assess an individual's mental and physical condition to determine whether they are incapacitated and in need of a guardian. This involves a comprehensive evaluation of the individual's medical and mental health status that includes a review of the individual's medical history, a physical examination, and a cognitive evaluation. The committee may also review the individual's medications, living arrangements, and financial status to gain a better understanding of their overall condition.

Each member of the committee is required to meet specific qualifications to ensure that they are qualified to evaluate the individual's medical and mental health status.

The physician on the committee must be licensed to practice medicine in Florida and have experience in treating individuals with the type of condition being evaluated. For example, if the individual is being evaluated for dementia, the physician on the committee should have experience in treating patients with dementia.

The psychiatrist or psychologist on the committee must also be licensed to practice in Florida and have experience in evaluating and treating individuals with mental health conditions. The individual must hold a doctoral degree in psychology or psychiatry and be trained in the evaluation of mental health disorders.

The layperson on the committee is typically an individual with experience in caring for individuals with the type of condition being evaluated. For example, if the individual is being evaluated for dementia, the layperson on the committee may be a social worker or caregiver with experience in caring for individuals with dementia.

In addition to meeting the specific qualifications for their respective roles, each member of the Examining Committee must also have a clear understanding of the criteria for determining incapacity in Florida. This includes an understanding of the legal process, the documentation required, and

3. Appointment Process: Steps and Requirements

the role of the Examining Committee in the process.

In Florida, the examination process typically includes the following:

1. **Medical evaluation:** The physician on the Examining Committee will evaluate the individual's medical history, review any medical records, and perform a physical examination. This evaluation will help to determine the individual's overall health status and any medical conditions that may be impacting their ability to care for themselves.

2. **Psychiatric or psychological evaluation:** The psychiatrist or psychologist on the Examining Committee will evaluate the individual's mental health status. This evaluation may include a cognitive assessment, a review of the individual's psychiatric history, and an evaluation of their behavior and emotional state.

3. **Functional evaluation:** The layperson on the Examining Committee will evaluate the individual's ability to care for themselves. This evaluation may include an assessment of the individual's ability to manage

their daily activities, such as bathing, dressing, and preparing meals.

After the examination, the Examining Committee will prepare a report detailing their findings and recommendations. The report is submitted to the court, and the information it contains is used to make a determination of capacity and the appropriateness of the appointment of a guardian, if necessary.

The Examining Committee evaluation report must include the following specific information:

1. **Identification of the individual being evaluated:** The report must include the individual's name, date of birth, and any other relevant identifying information.

2. **Basis for the evaluation:** The report must include a description of the reason for the evaluation, including any specific concerns or issues that prompted the evaluation.

3. **Evaluation findings:** The report must include the findings of each member of the Examining Committee, including the physician, the psychiatrist or psychologist, and the layperson. The report should provide a clear and detailed description of the

3. Appointment Process: Steps and Requirements

individual's mental and physical condition.

4. **Diagnosis and prognosis:** The report should include a diagnosis of the individual's condition and a prognosis for their future health and well-being.

5. **Recommendations:** The report should include specific recommendations for the individual's care and treatment, including any medications or therapies that may be necessary.

6. **Conclusion:** The report should conclude with a summary of the Examining Committee's findings and recommendations, as well as any other relevant information. *A sample Report of Examining Committee is attached in Appendix 2.*

In Florida, the evaluation report prepared by the Examining Committee is valid for 90 days from the date of the report. If the determination of incapacity is made based on the evaluation report, a guardian may be appointed to assist the individual with decision-making and care. However, the individual or another interested party may challenge the determination of incapacity and request a re-evaluation or renewal of the evaluation report.

Family and Professional Guardianship

If a re-evaluation or renewal is requested, the Examining Committee will conduct a new evaluation of the individual's mental and physical condition. The committee will follow the same examination process as before and prepare a new evaluation report detailing their findings and recommendations.

The requirements for re-evaluation and renewal of the evaluation report in Florida include the following:

1. **Request for re-evaluation or renewal:** A request for re-evaluation or renewal must be made in writing to the court. The request must provide a specific reason for the re-evaluation or renewal and be supported by evidence.

2. **Evaluation process:** The Examining Committee will conduct a new evaluation of the individual's mental and physical condition. The committee will follow the same examination process as before, which may include a review of the individual's medical history, physical examination, and cognitive evaluation.

3. **Renewal of report:** If the Examining Committee determines that the individual is still incapacitated, they will prepare a new

evaluation report. The report will include updated findings and recommendations, based on the new examination.

Re-evaluation of the report: If the Examining Committee determines that the individual is no longer incapacitated, they will prepare a new evaluation report. The report will include updated findings and recommendations, based on the new examination.

Court hearing: The new evaluation report will be submitted to the court for review. The court will schedule a hearing to review the report and determine whether the determination of incapacity should be revoked or maintained.

3.3.1.3 Appealing a Determination of Incapacity

If the Examining Committee determines that an individual is incapacitated, they may file a petition with the court to appoint a guardian. However, the individual or other interested parties may also contest the determination of incapacity and request a hearing.

At the hearing, the individual and any interested parties will have the opportunity to present evidence and argue against the determination of incapacity. The court will consider all evidence and will make a determination about whether the individual is incapacitated.

An individual may choose to appeal a determination of incapacity for a variety of reasons. Examples of potential grounds for appeal for a determination of incapacity in Florida may include:

1. **Errors in the evaluation process:** The Examining Committee may make mistakes during the evaluation process, such as failing to consider all relevant evidence or not following proper procedures. If an individual believes that there were significant errors in the evaluation process, they may have grounds for an appeal.

2. **Failure to consider all relevant evidence:** The Examining Committee may overlook important evidence that is relevant to the determination of incapacity. If an individual feels that not all relevant evidence was considered, they may choose to appeal the determination in order to ensure that all relevant evidence is evaluated.

3. **Disputes over the appointment of a guardian:** In some cases, an individual or their loved ones may disagree with the appointment of a specific guardian. If an individual feels that the appointed guardian is not appropriate or trustworthy, they may choose to appeal the determination in order to challenge the appointment of the guardian.

4. **Lack of due process:** An individual may choose to appeal a determination of incapacity if they feel that their legal rights were violated during the determination process. For example, if an individual was not given proper notice of the evaluation or was not allowed to present their own evidence, they may have grounds for an appeal.

5. **Conflicts of interest:** If there are conflicts of interest or bias present in the determination process, an individual may choose to appeal the decision. For example, if a member of the Examining Committee has a personal relationship with the appointed guardian, this may be considered a conflict of interest that could affect the outcome of the determination.

There are several reasons why an individual may choose to appeal a determination of incapacity.

One common reason is that the individual disagrees with the finding of incapacity and believes that they *are* capable of managing their own affairs. If an individual feels that they have been wrongly declared incapacitated, they may choose to appeal the decision in order to challenge the determination.

In some cases, the court may appoint a guardian that the individual or their family members do not trust or feel comfortable with. If this occurs, an individual may choose to appeal the determination in order to challenge the appointment of the guardian.

Finally, an individual may choose to appeal a determination of incapacity because they are concerned about losing their independence and autonomy. Significant consequences can result from a declaration of incapacity, such as the appointment of a guardian and restrictions on decision-making. If an individual believes that they are capable of managing their own affairs, they may choose to appeal the determination in order to preserve their independence and autonomy.

In Florida, the process for filing an appeal of a determination of incapacity involves submitting a written notice of appeal to the appropriate court within 30 days of the entry of the order of

3. Appointment Process: Steps and Requirements

incapacity. The notice of appeal must include the specific grounds for the appeal and must be served on all parties involved in the case.

In addition to the notice of appeal, the individual appealing the determination of incapacity must also file a record on appeal with the court. The record on appeal should include all relevant evidence, documents, and transcripts from the initial determination of incapacity hearing.

An appeal of a determination of incapacity must be filed with the appropriate district court of appeals. The specific court will depend on the location of the lower court that issued the determination of incapacity. It is important to consult with an attorney or review the court's website to determine the appropriate court to file the appeal with.

There are fees associated with filing an appeal of a determination of incapacity in Florida. The fees can vary depending on the specific court and the type of appeal being filed. Generally, the fees can range from several hundred to several thousand dollars.

In some cases, individuals may qualify for fee waivers or reduced fees based on their financial circumstances. Note that in addition to the court fees, there may be additional costs associated with filing an appeal, such as the cost of hiring an attorney or the cost of obtaining additional evidence or documentation.

The standard of review that the court will use when considering an appeal of a determination of incapacity in Florida will depend on the type of appeal being filed. There are two main types of appeals: **appeals of law** and **appeals of fact**.

When an **appeal of law** is filed, the appellate court will review the lower court's decision *de novo*, which means that the appellate court will give no deference to the lower court's decision and will review the case from scratch. This standard of review applies to questions of law, such as whether the lower court applied the correct legal standard when making its determination of incapacity.

When an **appeal of fact** is filed, the appellate court will review the lower court's decision based on the standard of review known as abuse of discretion. This standard of review means that the appellate court will give deference to the lower court's factual findings and will only overturn the lower court's decision if it finds that the lower court abused its discretion in making its determination of incapacity.

3. Appointment Process: Steps and Requirements

An abuse of discretion occurs when the lower court's decision is not based on the evidence presented or when it is clearly erroneous or unsupported by the evidence.

In some cases, the appellate court may use a mixed standard of review, which means that it will apply the appropriate standard of review to each issue raised on appeal.

When reviewing an appeal of a determination of incapacity in Florida, the court will consider several factors, including:

1. **Compliance with procedural requirements:** The court will consider whether all necessary procedures were followed in the initial determination of incapacity and whether proper notice was given to all parties involved.

   Sufficiency of the evidence: The court will review the evidence presented in the initial determination of incapacity to determine whether it supports the finding of incapacity.

   Use of proper legal standards: The court will consider whether the lower court applied the correct legal standards when making its determination of incapacity.

Credibility of witnesses: The court may evaluate the credibility of witnesses who provided evidence in the initial determination of incapacity.

Constitutionality of the determination: The court may consider whether the determination of incapacity violates an individual's constitutional rights.

Appointment of a guardian: If a guardian has been appointed, the court may consider whether the appointment was appropriate and whether the guardian is acting in the best interests of the individual.

The court's review of the appeal will depend on the specific issues raised on appeal and the type of appeal being filed. If the appeal is based on errors of law, the court will review the legal issues de novo. If the appeal is based on errors of fact, the court will review the factual findings for an abuse of discretion.

In an appeal of a determination of incapacity, the discovery and the evidence-gathering process is critical to building a strong case. During the

3. Appointment Process: Steps and Requirements

appeals process, both parties will have the opportunity to gather evidence and present arguments to support their position.

Discovery is the process by which both parties exchange information and evidence in the case. This can include documents, witness statements, expert reports, and other types of evidence. During discovery, each party may also request depositions, which are sworn statements from witnesses or parties involved in the case. Discovery allows both parties to fully evaluate the evidence and arguments presented by the other side.

In addition to discovery, each party may also file briefs with the appellate court outlining their legal arguments and the evidence they will present to support those arguments. The briefs must be submitted within specific timeframes established by the court.

It is worth mentioning that the scope of the evidence-gathering process in an appeal is more limited than in the initial determination of incapacity. The appellate court will not re-evaluate the evidence or make new factual findings, but will instead review the lower court's decision for errors of law or abuse of discretion.

In an appeal of a determination of incapacity, the types of evidence that may be presented are

Family and Professional Guardianship

similar to those presented in the initial determination of incapacity. However, the rules surrounding the admissibility of evidence may be different in the appeals process.

Evidence that may be presented in an appeal of a determination of incapacity includes medical records, witness statements, expert reports, and any other documentation that may be relevant to the issues raised on appeal. The specific types of evidence that may be presented will depend on the issues raised on appeal and the standard of review being applied.

One key difference between the evidence presented in the initial determination of incapacity and the evidence presented in the appeals process is that the parties may not be able to present new evidence that was not presented in the lower court. In general, the appellate court will only consider the evidence that was presented in the lower court and will not consider new evidence or testimony that was not previously presented.

In addition to the types of evidence that may be presented, the rules surrounding the admissibility of evidence may be different in the appeals process. The appellate court will consider whether the lower court followed the proper rules of evidence when admitting or excluding

3. Appointment Process: Steps and Requirements

evidence in the initial determination of incapacity.

The rules of evidence in the appeals process may be more relaxed than in the lower court, but they still require that the evidence presented be relevant and reliable. The appellate court may exclude evidence that is unfairly prejudicial or that does not meet the standard of relevance.

While an appeal of determination of incapacity in Florida is typically resolved through a court decision, there may be instances in which mediation or settlement can be a viable option.

Mediation or settlement can be beneficial because it allows the parties to work together to reach a resolution, particularly when the issues in the appeal are complex or emotionally charged. They can also work to avoid the time and expense of a full appeal and can lead to a mutually agreeable resolution.

Mediation is a process in which a neutral third-party mediator facilitates negotiations between the parties to reach a mutually acceptable agreement. Mediation can be a useful tool because it allows the parties to work together to find a solution that meets each of their needs and preferences.

Settlement is a process in which the parties agree to resolve the appeal without going to trial. Settlement can involve the parties agreeing to a specific outcome, such as the appointment of a new guardian, or agreeing to a modification of the original determination of incapacity.

The mediation process typically begins with the parties selecting a mediator who is trained and experienced in helping parties resolve disputes. The mediator will then schedule a mediation session, which is typically held in a neutral location.

At the mediation session, the parties and their attorneys will have the opportunity to present their arguments and evidence to the mediator. The mediator will then work with the parties to identify areas of agreement and disagreement and facilitate negotiations to reach a resolution.

Throughout the mediation process, the mediator may meet with the parties separately and together to help them explore potential solutions and work through any disputes or disagreements. The mediator may also make suggestions for ways to resolve the dispute, but the ultimate decision about whether to accept a settlement offer or resolution rests with the parties.

3. Appointment Process: Steps and Requirements

If the parties are able to reach an agreement through mediation, the mediator will draft a written settlement agreement that outlines the terms of the agreement. The parties will then sign the settlement agreement, and it will become binding and enforceable.

A trial for an appeal of a determination of incapacity in Florida is a formal proceeding in which the parties present their arguments and evidence to a judge or panel of judges. During the trial, the judge will hear testimony from witnesses, review evidence, and make a decision about the issues raised on appeal.

The trial will typically begin with opening statements from the parties, during which each side will present an overview of their case and the evidence they plan to present. The party appealing the determination of incapacity will present their case first, followed by the other party.

After opening statements, the parties will present their evidence and testimony. This may include medical records, witness statements, expert reports, and any other documentation that may be relevant to the issues raised on appeal.

During the presentation of evidence, both parties will have the opportunity to cross-examine witnesses and challenge the evidence presented by the other side. The judge may also ask questions of the witnesses and parties to clarify any issues or inconsistencies.

Once all of the evidence has been presented, by the parties, the judge will review the evidence presented and make a decision about the issues raised on appeal. The judge may issue a written decision or provide a ruling from the bench.

In a trial for an appeal of a determination of incapacity in Florida, there are several key players with distinct roles: the judge, the plaintiff, and the defendant.

The **judge** is responsible for overseeing the trial and making a decision about the issues raised on appeal. The judge is a neutral third party who is not affiliated with either the plaintiff or the defendant. The judge will consider the evidence presented by both sides, evaluate the legal arguments, and make a ruling based on the law and the facts of the case.

The **plaintiff** is the party who is appealing the determination of incapacity. The plaintiff is typically represented by an attorney, who will present the evidence and legal arguments on behalf of the plaintiff. The plaintiff's goal is to convince

3. Appointment Process: Steps and Requirements

the judge that the lower court's decision was incorrect and that the determination of incapacity should be overturned.

The **defendant** is the party who is opposing the appeal. The defendant may be the proposed guardian or another interested party, such as a family member or healthcare provider. The defendant is also typically represented by an attorney, who will present the evidence and legal arguments on behalf of the defendant. The defendant's goal is to convince the judge that the lower court's decision was correct, and that the determination of incapacity should be upheld.

In addition to these key players, there may be other individuals involved in the trial, such as witnesses who can testify about the individual's capacity, medical professionals who can provide expert testimony, or family members who can provide insight into the individual's personal life.

The possible outcomes of a trial for an appeal of a determination of incapacity in Florida depend on the issues raised on appeal and the evidence presented. The judge may rule in favor of the plaintiff, in which case the determination of incapacity will be overturned and a new determination may be made, or the judge may rule in favor of the defendant, in which case the determination of incapacity will be upheld.

If the judge rules in favor of the plaintiff and overturns the determination of incapacity, the case will typically be remanded to the lower court for further proceedings. The parties may need to go through the process of determining incapacity again, and a new guardian may be appointed if necessary.

If the judge rules in favor of the defendant and upholds the determination of incapacity, the plaintiff may have the option to appeal the decision to a higher court. If the decision is not appealed, the lower court's determination of incapacity will remain in place, and the proposed guardian or other interested party will continue to serve in that role.

The trial process can be time-consuming and expensive, and the outcome is never guaranteed. For this reason, many individuals choose to work with an experienced attorney to evaluate the potential risks and benefits of appealing a determination of incapacity, and to ensure that their case is presented effectively during the trial.

3.3.2. Filing a Petition for Guardianship

Any interested party can file a petition for guardianship. This includes family members, friends, caregivers, and other individuals who have knowledge of the individual's condition and believe that a guardian is necessary.

The petition must be filed in the county where the individual in need of a guardian resides and must include information about the individual's condition and the reasons why a guardian is necessary.

3.3.2.1. Notice Requirements

Notice is the formal process of informing interested parties about a legal proceeding, such as a hearing or trial. Proper notice is necessary to ensure that all interested parties have an opportunity to participate in the legal process and to protect their rights.

In guardianship proceedings in Florida, notice requirements are an essential aspect of the legal process because they can have significant implications for the individual in question and their loved ones. For example, a determination of incapacity may result in the appointment of a guardian who will have significant decision-making authority over the individual's life.

In guardianship proceedings, notice is particularly important because of the outcome of the proceeding.

In Florida guardianship proceedings, certain individuals must receive notice to ensure that they have an opportunity to participate in the legal process and to protect their interests. The following are individuals who must receive notice in a guardianship proceeding:

1. **The alleged incapacitated person:** The alleged incapacitated person must receive notice of the guardianship proceeding to ensure that they have an opportunity to participate in the process and to protect their rights.

   The alleged incapacitated person's spouse: The alleged incapacitated person's spouse must receive notice of the guardianship proceeding, even if they are separated or divorced.

   The alleged incapacitated person's adult children: The alleged incapacitated person's adult children must receive notice of the guardianship proceeding.

The alleged incapacitated person's parents: The alleged incapacitated person's parents must receive notice of the guardianship proceeding if they are living and have not been adjudicated incapacitated.

The proposed guardian: The proposed guardian must receive notice of the guardianship proceeding to ensure that they have an opportunity to participate in the process and to protect their interests.

Any person who has filed a request for notice: Any person who has filed a request for notice with the court must receive notice of the guardianship proceeding.

Exceptions to the notice requirement may apply in certain circumstances. For example, if the court determines that providing notice would be detrimental to the alleged incapacitated person's health or welfare, it may waive the notice requirement. However, waivers of notice are relatively rare and are only granted in exceptional circumstances.

The following information must be included in the notice:

1. **Date, time, and location of the hearing:** The notice must include the date, time, and location of the hearing to ensure that interested parties know when and where to appear.

   Nature of the proceeding: The notice must specify that the proceeding concerns a guardianship and include the name of the alleged incapacitated person and the name of the proposed guardian.

   Contact information for the court: The notice must include contact information for the court, including the name and address of the court, the telephone number, and the case number.

   Information about the right to be heard: The notice must include information about the right to be heard and the right to object to guardianship.

   Language and format requirements: The notice must be written in clear, concise language that is easy to understand. The notice must also be in a format that is accessible to all interested parties, including those with disabilities or limited English proficiency.

Consequences of failure to appear: The notice must include information about the consequences of failure to appear, such as the possibility of a default judgment or the appointment of a guardian without objection.

It is important to ensure that the notice is accurate and complete to avoid any confusion or misunderstandings.

Failure to provide proper notice or to include all the necessary information in the notice can result in delays or errors in the legal process. In some cases, failure to provide proper notice may also result in the nullification of the entire proceeding.

Notice must be provided within specific timelines to ensure that interested parties have sufficient time to prepare for the hearing and to protect their rights. Initial notice must be provided at least 14 days before the hearing. This is the first notice that is provided to interested parties to inform them of the guardianship proceeding and to give them sufficient time to prepare and protect their rights.

Family and Professional Guardianship

If an examining committee is appointed to evaluate the alleged incapacitated person, notice of the examination must be provided at least 72 hours before the examination.

Notice may be provided in a variety of ways, including personal service, mail, or email. Personal service is generally the most reliable method of providing notice, as it ensures that the notice is received by the intended recipient. However, if personal service is not possible, notice may be provided by mail or email.

In certain circumstances, notice of a guardianship proceeding may be waived. The waiver of notice is a legal document signed by an interested party indicating that they are aware of the guardianship proceeding and are waiving their right to receive notice.

- An interested party may choose to waive their right to receive notice voluntarily. This may occur, for example, if the interested party is unable to attend the hearing but wants to ensure that the proceeding moves forward.
- An interested party may waive their right to receive notice if they are fully informed of their rights and the consequences of waiving notice. The waiver

must be voluntary and made with knowledge of the right to receive notice and the consequences of waiving that right.

In some cases, notice may be deemed to have been waived. For example, if an interested party fails to attend the hearing after receiving proper notice, the court may deem that party to have waived their right to notice.

Waivers of notice are relatively rare and are only granted in exceptional circumstances. This is because notice is a critical aspect of the legal process, and ensuring that all interested parties are aware of the proceeding is essential to protecting their rights.

3.3.2.2. Filing Fees

In Florida, there are fees associated with filing a petition for guardianship. The filing fee varies depending on the county where the petition is filed. In addition to the filing fee, there may be additional costs associated with the appointment of a guardian, such as the cost of an attorney or other professional services.

The fees are generally made up of two parts: **court fees** and **attorney fees**.

- Court fees are set by the state and are the same across all counties.
- Attorney fees vary depending on the attorney's hourly rate and the complexity of the case. It is advisable to consult with an attorney who is experienced in guardianship proceedings in Florida first to determine the exact amount of their fees.

In addition to the filing fee, there may be other costs associated with a guardianship proceeding, such as fees for expert evaluations, court-appointed attorneys, and court reporters. The court may order the petitioner to pay for the incapacitated person's attorney fees, if necessary. These costs can add up quickly and should be taken into consideration when deciding whether to initiate a guardianship proceeding.

In some circumstances, a fee waiver may be granted to a petitioner who is unable to pay the required fees for initiating a guardianship proceeding in Florida. A fee waiver is designed to ensure that all parties have access to the court system, regardless of their ability to pay.

To be eligible for a fee waiver, the petitioner must demonstrate that they are indigent and unable to pay the required fees. This typically requires the petitioner to provide detailed information about their income and expenses. The court will

3. Appointment Process: Steps and Requirements

review this information and determine whether the petitioner is eligible for a fee waiver.

If the court determines that the petitioner is eligible for a fee waiver, the filing fees and other associated costs may be waived or reduced. Even if a fee waiver is granted, the petitioner may still be responsible for other costs associated with the guardianship proceeding, such as fees for expert evaluations or court-appointed attorneys.

In addition to fee waivers, some counties in Florida have established programs that provide reduced fees for certain types of guardianship proceedings. These programs are designed to make guardianship more accessible and affordable for low-income individuals and families.

Additionally, in some cases, the court may appoint an attorney to represent the alleged incapacitated person or other parties in the proceeding. The cost of this attorney may be the responsibility of the petitioner or may be borne by the incapacitated person, the estate, or the court.

Other costs can include court reporter fees, transcription fees, and other costs associated with the production of transcripts of court proceedings. These costs are rare in initial guardian petitions.

Family and Professional Guardianship

Often, guardian fees are an overlooked cost. These are fees that guardians receive for their services to and on behalf of the incapacitated person appointed to the guardian. These fees are designed to compensate guardians for their time and effort in carrying out their guardian responsibilities.

The types of fees that a guardian is entitled to receive will depend on the specific circumstances of the case. These may include fees for services rendered, reimbursement for expenses incurred, and compensation for lost wages or income.

These fees can be a flat fee for services (a one-time fee) but are usually billed per hour for services rendered on behalf of the incapacitated person. You should be aware that if the proposed guardian is appointed, they will be entitled to fees incurred while going through the petition and appointment process.

All guardian fee invoices must be approved by the court and signed by the judge presiding over the case. Guardian fees may include:

- **Fees for services rendered** - These fees are typically paid on an hourly basis and are designed to compensate the guardian for the time spent carrying out their duties. The hourly rate will depend on the complexity of the case and the experience of the guardian. The allowed fees in Florida range from $65.00 per hour to $175.00 per hour depending on the county.

- **Reimbursement for expenses incurred** - These expenses may include travel expenses, costs for expert evaluations, and any other expenses that are reasonably necessary for the guardian to carry out their responsibilities.

- **Compensation for lost wages, travel or income.** This type of fee is designed to compensate the guardian for any income they may lose as a result of taking on the role of guardian. The amount of compensation will depend on the guardian's income prior to taking on the role of guardian and the amount of time spent carrying out their duties.

3.3.2.3. Preparing the Petition

To file a petition for guardianship, the petitioner must prepare several documents and file them with the court.

Petition for guardianship. This document provides information about the individual in need of a guardian, as well as the reasons why the petitioner believes a guardian is necessary.

The purpose of the petition is to establish that the alleged incapacitated person needs a guardian. The petition must explain why the petitioner believes a guardian is necessary and the specific powers that the guardian is being asked to assume.

The petition must include:

- **The name and address of the alleged incapacitated person**, as well as their age and the county in which they reside.

- **Detailed information about the alleged incapacity**, including the nature of the incapacity, how long it has existed, and any medical evidence or evaluations that support the assertion.

- **The specific powers that the guardian is being asked to assume**, such as the power to make medical decisions or the power to manage the alleged incapacitated person's finances.

3. Appointment Process: Steps and Requirements

- **The identity of the proposed guardian** and provide information about their qualifications, including any relevant education or experience.

- **A statement of any objections** or potential conflicts of interest.

- **Oath of the petitioner.** This document is a sworn statement that the information provided in the petition is true and accurate.

The Oath of the Petitioner should be signed and dated by the petitioner and notarized. The petitioner should read the document carefully before signing and ensure that the information provided in the petition is accurate and truthful.

By signing the Oath of the Petitioner, the petitioner is affirming that they understand the serious nature of the petition for guardianship and are willing to provide all necessary information to the court. A Sample Petition for Guardian Form is provided in Appendix 3.

- **Designation of resident agent.** This document provides the name and contact information of a resident agent who can be contacted if the petitioner is unavailable.

The purpose of the designation of resident agent is to ensure that the court can communicate with the petitioner or the petitioner's representative. The document should include the name and contact information of the resident agent, who should be located in the same county as the petitioner.

The resident agent should be informed of their role and responsibilities and should be willing to act as the point of contact between the court and the petitioner.

- **Notice of hearing.** This document provides notice of the hearing date, time, and location, as well as the reasons why a guardian is being sought.

It is highly recommended for a petitioner to hire an attorney who can guide them through the guardianship appointment process. A representing attorney can prepare the necessary documents and make sure that all legal requirements are met.

3.3.2.4. Finding a Representing Attorney

Finding a representing attorney is an important step in the process of appointing a guardian. A representing attorney is an attorney who represents the petitioner in the guardianship appointment process. The attorney can help the petitioner navigate the legal process and ensure that all legal requirements are met.

The attorney can also provide advice on the best course of action and help ensure that the individual in need of a guardian is properly cared for. In addition, the attorney will ensure that the petitioner prepares the necessary documents and presents evidence in court.

There are several ways to find a representing attorney in Florida, including:

1. **Referrals from friends, family, or other professionals:** You can ask for recommendations from people you know or professionals who work with individuals who may need a guardian, such as social workers, doctors, or financial advisors.

2. **Online searches:** You can search online for attorneys who specialize in guardianship and elder law in your area.

3. **Bar Association referrals:** You can contact the Florida Bar Association for referrals to attorneys who specialize in guardianship and elder law.

4. **Legal aid organizations:** You may be eligible for assistance from a legal aid organization if you have a low income or meet other eligibility requirements.

Questions you should ask a prospective attorney:

1. How many guardian cases have you represented?
2. How many years have you been working in this area?
3. In what counties do you represent guardians?
4. Do you represent elder law cases?
5. Do you represent probate cases?
6. How many other guardians do you represent?
7. What is your fee structure?
8. Are you licensed to practice in Florida?

When choosing a representing attorney, it is important to consider their experience and expertise in guardianship and elder law. You should also

3. Appointment Process: Steps and Requirements

consider their availability and communication style, as well as their fees and billing practices.

In Florida, representing attorneys charge fees based on either an hourly rate or a flat fee. The fee will depend on the complexity of the case and the amount of work required.

Once you have found a representing attorney, it is important to work closely with them throughout the guardianship appointment process. The attorney can help you prepare the necessary documents, present evidence in court, and advocate for the best interests of the individual in need of a guardian.

You should be prepared to provide the attorney with all necessary information, including medical records, financial statements, and other relevant documents. You should also be prepared to attend court hearings and provide testimony or evidence as needed.

3.4. Chapter Summary

The guardianship appointment process in Florida is supposed to provide for the care and protection of individuals who are no longer capable of making their own decisions. The process involves several steps, including determining incapacity, filing a petition for guardianship, assessment by the examining committee, court hearings and decision-making, and finding a representing attorney.

The determination of incapacity is the first step in the guardianship appointment process. It involves an evaluation of the individual's ability to make decisions and care for themselves. The criteria for determining incapacity in Florida includes the individual's ability to understand and appreciate consequences, manage their own affairs, and the presence of mental or physical incapacity.

A mental or physical incapacity refers to the individual's inability to perform the daily tasks necessary to care for themselves or make important decisions, which could include a medical diagnosis, a disability, or the result of an accident or injury.

The petitioner must file a petition for guardianship with the court. This document provides information about the individual in need of a guardian, as well as the reasons why a guardian is necessary. The petitioner must also file an Oath of the Petitioner, which is a sworn statement that the information provided in the petition is true and accurate. Additionally, the petitioner must file a designation of resident

3. Appointment Process: Steps and Requirements

agent, which provides the name and contact information of a resident agent who can be contacted if the petitioner is unavailable.

Once the petition is filed, the court will set a hearing date and provide notice of the hearing to all interested parties. This notice must include the hearing date, time, and location, as well as the reasons why a guardian is being sought. Notice must be provided to the individual in need of a guardian, as well as any other interested parties, such as family members or friends.

As part of the guardianship appointment process in Florida, an examining committee is appointed to evaluate the individual in need of a guardian. The committee consists of three members, including a physician, a mental health professional, and a layperson who has experience working with individuals who are incapacitated. The committee will evaluate the individual's ability to make decisions and care for themselves and will provide a written report to the court.

The report provided by the examining committee is a critical component of the guardianship appointment process in Florida. It must include specific information about the individual's physical and mental condition, their ability to make decisions, and any other relevant factors. The report must also include recommendations for the type of guardianship that is necessary, including the scope of the guardian's authority and the specific areas in which the guardian will make decisions.

If the court determines that a guardian is necessary, the court will appoint a guardian to care for the individual. The guardian is responsible for making decisions on behalf of the individual, including decisions related to medical treatment, housing, and financial matters. In some cases, the guardian may be a family member or friend who is already familiar with the individual's needs and preferences. However, in other cases, a court-appointed guardian may be necessary to ensure that the individual's best interests are being served.

In order to ensure that the process is carried out in a fair, transparent, and compassionate manner, it is important to follow the guidelines and procedures for each step of the process. This includes ensuring that the ward's rights are protected, their voice is heard, and they are treated with respect and dignity throughout the process.

The guardianship appointment process can be complex and time-consuming, and it may

3. Appointment Process: Steps and Requirements

involve the cooperation of family members or other interested parties. However, by working together and following the guidelines and procedures, the best interests of the ward can be served and their needs can be met.

It is also important to recognize that the guardianship appointment process is not a one-time event. The court will periodically review the guardian's performance and may modify or terminate the guardianship if it is no longer necessary. This ensures that the ward's needs continue to be met over time and that their rights are protected.

By having a thorough understanding of the guardianship appointment process, you can help ensure that people are protected and cared for and that their rights and interests are always prioritized. Whether you are a guardian, healthcare professional, or family member, I hope that the information provided in this chapter will come in handy if you need to navigate the guardianship appointment process in Florida.

4. Guardian Compensation in Florida

4.1. Overview

I could not have written a book about guardianship in Florida without dedicating a full chapter to the topic of guardian compensation. Without denying that care providers can have non-financial motivations, it is reasonable to assume that guardian compensation is important in ensuring that the system works effectively and that individuals who require a guardian receive high-quality care and support.

One reason for this is that the role of a guardian can be demanding and time-consuming, and the compensation provided to a guardian can help to offset the costs of serving in this role. A guardian is responsible for making decisions on behalf of another person who cannot make these decisions for themselves. This can involve a wide range of tasks, including managing finances, making healthcare decisions, and providing daily care and support.

By the end of this chapter, readers will have a better understanding of the role and importance of fair and adequate compensation for guardians and the sources of funds to pay this compensation. This can help to ensure that individuals who require a guardian are provided with the best possible care and support, and that qualified individuals are willing and able to serve as guardians.

What is Guardian Compensation? This refers to the complex system of court filings, court approvals, financial record keeping, and reporting. It includes the sources and amount of a Ward's estate and a system of payment or reimbursements provided to an individual, appointed by a court, to act as a legal guardian for another person who is unable to manage their own affairs.

This compensation may include a variety of expenses related to the duties of the guardian, such as fees for legal and accounting services, travel expenses, and compensation for the guardian's time and effort in carrying out their responsibilities.

4. Guardian Compensation in Florida

The amount and type of compensation may vary depending on the jurisdiction, the type of guardian, and the needs of the person under guardianship. The goal of guardian compensation is to ensure that qualified individuals are willing and able to act as guardians and have the resources necessary to provide high-quality care and support to the person under their care.

Without adequate compensation, individuals may be reluctant to serve as a guardian, especially if the guardianship requires a significant amount of time, effort, and resources. In addition, guardianship can involve complex legal and financial matters, and the compensation provided to a guardian can help to cover the cost of hiring professional services such as attorneys and accountants to assist with these matters.

In some cases, guardians may need to travel, take time off from work, or make other sacrifices to carry out their duties, and compensation can help offset these costs. Furthermore, compensated guardians are more likely to be motivated and committed to providing high-quality care to the person under their guardianship.

Adequate compensation for guardians is essential in attracting and retaining qualified individuals who are willing to undertake the important responsibility of serving as a guardian.

Guardian of the person and guardian of the property are two main types of guardianship in Florida:

- A **guardian of the person** is responsible for making decisions related to the health, welfare, and personal care of the individual under guardianship.

- A **guardian of the property** is responsible for managing the financial affairs of the individual under guardianship.

Florida law allows for both professional and family guardians to serve in these roles, and the compensation and responsibilities of the guardian will vary depending on the type of guardianship and the needs of the individual under guardianship.

4.2. Professional Guardians

4.2.1. Compensation Options

Florida Statute 744.108 discusses the compensation of a guardian. Compensation for professional guardians in Florida may take a variety of forms, including hourly or flat fee compensation, reimbursement for expenses, allowances and stipends, and other miscellaneous compensation.

Each type of compensation has specific requirements and limits that must be followed in order to ensure compliance with legal and ethical guidelines.

4.2.1.1. Hourly and Flat Fee Compensation for Professional Guardians

Hourly compensation involves payment for the time spent working on behalf of the person under guardianship, while flat fee compensation involves payment of a fixed amount for a specific period, such as a month or a year.

The average annual salary for the guardianship jobs category in Florida is $44,750. This translates to an hourly rate of approximately $21.51, a weekly income of $860, or a monthly income of $3,729.

While the Florida statutes only requires that guardian fees be reasonable, most court jurisdictions have established administrative regulations that cap guardian fees. Some, like Orange County, cap them at $70 per hour while other counties use higher caps or complexity-based caps.

Hourly compensation is one of the most common forms of compensation for professional guardians in Florida. Under this type of compensation, the guardian is paid a set hourly rate for the time spent working on behalf of the person under guardianship. Hourly rates may vary depending on a variety of factors, including the complexity of the case, the experience of the guardian, and the geographic location of the case.

Hourly compensation may be advantageous for professional guardians who work on cases with a high level of complexity or a large number of tasks to be completed. More specifically, hourly compensation allows the guardian to be paid for the time spent on these tasks, which can be a fair and transparent way of compensating for the work performed. Hourly compensation may also be advantageous for the person under guardianship, as it ensures that the guardian is only paid for the time spent on their case.

Flat fee compensation is another common type of compensation available to professional guardians in Florida. Under this type of compensation, the guardian is paid a fixed amount for a specific period of time, such as a month or a year. Flat fee compensation may be more advantageous for cases that have a lower level of complexity or a limited number of tasks to be completed.

Flat fee compensation means the guardian will be paid a fixed amount, regardless of the amount of time spent on the case. This can be advantageous for both the guardian and the person under guardianship, as it ensures that the guardian is compensated for their work, regardless of the amount of time spent on the case.

In addition to hourly and flat fee compensation, other types of compensation may be available, including reimbursement for expenses, allowances and stipends, and other miscellaneous compensation, depending on the specific case and the needs of the person under guardianship.

4.2.1.2. Reimbursement for Expenses for Professional Guardians

Reimbursement for expenses is an important aspect of compensation, as it ensures that guardians are able to provide high-quality care and support without incurring undue financial burdens.

There are a variety of expenses that may be reimbursed. These may include expenses related to travel, lodging, meals, and other necessary expenses. For example, a guardian may be reimbursed for expenses related to travel to court hearings, meetings with healthcare providers or other professionals, or other necessary events.

In order to be eligible for reimbursement, expenses must be directly related to the work performed on behalf of the person under guardianship. Expenses must also be reasonable and necessary and must be documented and reported in accordance with legal and ethical guidelines.

To document and report expenses, guardians must keep careful records of all expenses incurred, including receipts, invoices, and other documentation. These records must be detailed and accurate, and must clearly demonstrate the relationship between the expenses and the work performed on behalf of the person under guardianship.

Reimbursement for expenses may be subject to certain limits or restrictions, depending on the specific case and the needs of the person under guardianship. For example, there may be limits on the amount that can be reimbursed for specific types of expenses, or restrictions on the types of expenses that are eligible for reimbursement.

4.2.1.3. Allowances and Stipends for Professional Guardians

In order to be eligible for allowances and stipends, professional guardians in Florida must meet certain requirements. These requirements may include providing detailed documentation of the expenses incurred, obtaining prior approval for specific types of expenses or allowances, and ensuring compliance with legal and ethical guidelines.

4.2.2. Determination and Approval of Professional Guardian Compensation

The approval of professional guardian compensation is handled by the court system. The court will review and approve all compensation requests made by the professional guardian in order to ensure that they are reasonable and necessary for the work performed on behalf of the person under guardianship.

The court may also review and approve expenses related to the work performed by the professional guardian, such as travel expenses or expenses related to necessary equipment or supplies. These expenses must be documented and reported in accordance with legal and ethical guidelines and must be directly related to the work performed on behalf of the person under guardianship.

In addition to court approval, professional guardian compensation can also be subject to certain limitations or restrictions. For example, there can be limits on the amount of compensation that can be paid in a specific case, or restrictions on the types of expenses that are eligible for reimbursement.

4.3. Family Guardians
4.3.1. Compensation Options

In Florida, family members may be appointed as guardians for their loved ones who are incapacitated or otherwise unable to make their own decisions. Serving as a family guardian can be a challenging and rewarding experience, but it can also be time-consuming and emotionally draining. To help offset the costs and responsibilities associated with family guardianship, various types of compensation may be available to family guardians in Florida.

The court case Jones v. Guardianship of Jones, decided on February 14, 2020, in Florida, revolves around the question of whether the daughter of the ward should receive compensation for serving as her father's appointed guardian. Initially, the daughter's request for compensation was denied, with the court asserting that, as the ward's daughter, she had an obligation to provide these services without compensation. However, this decision was reversed and remanded by the 5th District Court of Appeal.

The appellate court determined that family member guardians are entitled to compensation for services that a professional or non-family member guardian would reasonably perform when discharging their duty to the ward. Family member guardians are not entitled to compensation for services that any family member might perform under similar circumstances, such as cleaning, cooking, and other household tasks. A family member guardian would, however, qualify for compensation for duties such as managing a ward's housing, medical and finances.

4.3.1.1. Hourly and Flat Fee Compensation for Family Guardians

Hourly and flat fee compensation models can also be used to pay family guardians for their time and effort in performing their duties as a guardian. The hourly rate will vary depending on the location, complexity, and length of the guardianship. Family guardians are typically required to keep detailed records of their time spent on guardianship duties, and to submit this information to the court for approval.

A flat fee compensation can be determined based on the specific needs of the person under guardianship and may vary depending on the complexity and length of the guardianship. Family guardians are typically required to submit a detailed proposal for the flat fee, outlining the specific services to be provided and the costs associated with those services.

Both hourly and flat fee compensation structures have their advantages and disadvantages for family guardians. Hourly compensation may provide more flexibility and freedom, as family guardians are able to charge for their time as they see fit. However, it may also be more difficult to track and document hours and may be subject to fluctuations in demand or work volume.

Flat fee compensation may provide more stability and predictability; it may also be more difficult to determine a fair and reasonable fee that adequately compensates family guardians for their time and effort.

In order to be eligible for hourly or flat fee compensation as a family guardian in Florida, there are certain requirements that must be met. These requirements can include obtaining court approval for compensation, maintaining detailed records of time spent on guardianship duties, and complying with legal and ethical guidelines related to compensation.

4.3.1.2. Reimbursement for Expenses for Family Guardians

Reimbursable expenses can include a wide range of costs, including medical and dental expenses, transportation costs, home modification expenses such as wheelchair ramps, walk-in tubs, and stair lifts, and other expenses related to the person's care and support. Family guardians can also be eligible for reimbursement of their own expenses, such as travel expenses or other costs associated with providing care and support to the person under guardianship.

The approval process for reimbursement of expenses can involve submitting detailed records of all expenses incurred, along with supporting documentation and receipts. The court will review and approve these records, in order to ensure that the expenses are reasonable and necessary for the care and support of the person under guardianship.

The same limitations and restrictions on reimbursement of expenses will potentially apply for family guardians as for any other type of guardian. For example, there may be limits on the types of expenses that are eligible for reimbursement, or restrictions on the total amount of reimbursement that can be provided in a specific case.

4.3.1.3. Miscellaneous Compensation for Family Guardians

Some examples of miscellaneous compensation that may be available to family guardians in Florida include legal fees, training, and education expenses, and fees for court-appointed attorneys or other professionals. These costs may be related to the guardianship itself or may be related to the family guardian's own personal development or support.

To be eligible for miscellaneous compensation as a family guardian, requirements that must be met include obtaining court approval for the compensation, maintaining detailed records of expenses and time spent on guardianship duties, and complying with legal and ethical guidelines related to compensation.

4.3.2. Determination and Approval of Compensation for Family Guardians

As already mentioned, the compensation available to guardians, both professional and family guardians, may vary depending on the specific circumstances of the guardianship case.

For family guardians in Florida, compensation may be determined on a case-by-case basis, based on the specific circumstances of the guardianship case. Family guardians may be eligible for reimbursement of expenses, hourly or flat fee compensation, allowances and stipends, and miscellaneous compensation, as discussed earlier.

4.4. Differences Between Compensation for Professional and Family Guardians in Florida

While the sections above highlight many similarities between the compensation plans available for professional and family guardians, there are, in fact, significant differences.

It is likely no surprise that professional guardians must meet certain educational requirements, which is not the case for family guardians. These requirements impact the types of compensation available to each type of guardian.

Specifically, in Florida, a professional guardian must complete a 40-hour initial training course approved by the Florida Department of Elder Affairs (DOEA).

In contrast, family guardians in Florida are not required to meet any specific educational requirements in order to serve as a guardian. However, having a basic understanding of the legal and ethical considerations related to guardianship will be helpful for family guardians in fulfilling their duties.

Because of the differences in educational requirements between family and professional guardians, the types of compensation available may also differ.

- Professional guardians may be able to command higher hourly or flat fee compensation, due to their specialized education and training.
- Family guardians are eligible for reimbursement of expenses related to their duties as a guardian, as well as hourly or flat fee compensation, allowances, stipends, and miscellaneous compensation.

There is one big advantage to family guardianship. Education and training are not the only factors that determine the effectiveness of a guardian. Family guardians who have a close personal relationship with the person under guardianship, in some cases, may be better equipped to provide emotional support and comfort, even if they do not have the same level of formal education and training as a professional guardian.

4.5. Source of Compensation for Professional and Family Guardians

Professional guardians and family guardians in Florida may be compensated for their services using the ward's assets. This means that the fees and expenses charged by the guardian will be paid from the ward's estate, which may include income, investments, property, and other assets.

It's important to note that the payment for guardian services is subject to court approval. The court will review the proposed fees and expenses and determine whether they are reasonable and necessary. If the court approves the payment, the guardian can then receive compensation from the ward's assets.

Chapter 744.108 of Florida Statutes provides guidance on how the compensation should be determined. In the case of professional guardians, the compensation must be reasonable and not exceed the value of the ward's estate. Family guardians are also entitled to compensation, but the compensation may not be greater than what a professional guardian would charge.

If the ward has no resources or assets, and there is no other source of funds available to pay for the guardian's services, the state of Florida may provide payment for the guardian's services. This only applies in the case of the Public Guardianship Program.

The state of Florida provides funding for the guardianship of persons who are indigent or otherwise unable to afford a guardian. A public guardian is a person or organization appointed by the Statewide Public Guardianship Office to serve as a guardian for those who have no family or friends available to serve as guardians.

This is a last resort and is only available when there is no other source of payment for the guardian's services. These funds are not paid to family or professional guardians, only to the public guardian service.

In order to qualify for such funding, the ward must be found to be indigent, meaning that the ward does not have sufficient income or assets to pay for the cost of guardianship. The court will consider various factors in making this determination, including the ward's income, assets, and expenses.

It's important to note that public funding is very limited, and not all wards who are indigent will be able to receive guardianship services. In some cases, the court may appoint a volunteer guardian or an unpaid family member to serve as the guardian, rather than using public funding.

Other than the Public Guardian Program, the state does not compensate guardians. If a guardian takes cases where there is no estate, meaning no money, then the guardian takes these cases as *pro bono*, in other words, they are not expecting to be compensated for cases where there are no assets or income.

4.6. Challenges and Ethical Considerations Associated with Guardian Compensation

There are several potential challenges and ethical considerations related to compensating guardians. These challenges and ethical considerations may be addressable by establishing clear guidelines for compensation practices and regularly reviewing and updating these guidelines. This can help ensure that compensation is fair and reasonable.

One potential challenge is the lack of standardization in compensation for professional guardians. Compensation rates can vary significantly depending on the complexity of the case and the time and effort required, which can make it difficult to determine fair compensation rates and may result in disparities in compensation between professional guardians.

Another challenge is the arguably limited funding for guardianship services in Florida, which can lead to inadequate compensation for guardians. The available funding is restricted to the Public Guardianship Service. This can make it difficult to attract and retain qualified guardians who can provide high-quality services to the individuals under their guardianship.

Additionally, expenses associated with carrying out guardianship responsibilities can be unpredictable and may vary significantly from case to case, which can make it difficult for guardians to plan and budget for expenses, resulting in additional financial burdens.

4. Guardian Compensation in Florida

One key ethical consideration that comes to mind is avoiding conflicts of interest. Guardians must ensure that they do not benefit personally from the compensation they receive - that compensation is not determined based on decisions that benefit them personally rather than the individuals under their guardianship.

Maintaining the integrity of the guardianship process is also important. Compensation practices should be determined based on the best interests of the individuals under guardianship, rather than personal gain. This helps to ensure that the guardianship process remains focused on the wellbeing of the individuals under guardianship. Additionally, guardians should not use their position to exploit the individuals under their guardianship for financial gain. Compensation should be fair and reasonable, and should not be excessive.

Guidelines and standards for compensation practices can ensure that these considerations are addressed when compensating professional and family guardians. A guideline should outline the types of compensation that are appropriate and the factors that should be considered when determining compensation rates.

Awareness of ethical considerations related to compensation can avoid many problems. Such awareness helps ensure that guardians are aware of their responsibilities and ethical obligations, and can make informed decisions when it comes to compensation.

4.7. Chapter Summary

Whether you are a professional guardian who has undergone specialized training and education, or a family guardian who is caring for a loved one, having a good understanding of the types and levels of compensation available to guardians in Florida can help you better navigate through the process of becoming a guardian or finding one.

I advise both professional and family guardians to familiarize themselves with all forms of compensation, including hourly and flat fee compensation, reimbursement for expenses, allowances, and miscellaneous compensation; such familiarity will make it easy to understand how each type of compensation might be applied in practice.

Fair and adequate compensation is essential to attract and retain qualified guardians who can provide high-quality services to the individuals under their guardianship. This applies to both family and professional guardians. Guardianship is a demanding and complex job that requires a significant amount of time, effort, and resources. Without fair and adequate compensation, it may be difficult to attract and retain qualified individuals to serve as guardians.

It ensures that guardians are compensated fairly for their time and expertise, which can help reduce turnover and improve the quality of care provided to individuals under guardianship. Inadequate compensation, on the other hand, may result in guardians cutting corners or not being able to provide the level of care that is needed.

Professional and family guardians in Florida can be compensated for their services using the ward's assets. This means that the fairness of compensation must be established by taking into account both the guardian's and the ward's needs. At times, a ward may not have any resource of assets, a situation that poses additional challenges to the issue of fair compensation.

Adequate compensation also allows guardians to meet the expenses associated with carrying out their responsibilities, such as travel, lodging, and legal fees. These expenses can add up quickly and can be a significant burden for guardians who are not adequately compensated.

In addition to fair and adequate compensation, it is also important to ensure that guardians are compensated ethically. This means that compensation should not be influenced by personal gain or other factors that may compromise the integrity of the guardianship process. Ethical compensation practices help maintain the trust and confidence of the individuals under guardianship and the public at large.

5. Governing Body & Guardianship Reporting in Florida

5.1. Overview

The purpose of this chapter is to provide a comprehensive overview of guardianship and the consequences of non-compliance with reporting requirements. I will start with a real case study. Then I will provide helpful information for completing and submitting guardianship reports and show you how to determine the reporting periods.

Guardianship reporting involves the submission of various reports by the guardian to the court and other governing bodies. In Florida, the guardianship process is overseen and regulated by several governing bodies, including the Office of Public and Professional Guardians, the Clerk of Court, and the Circuit Court Probate Division.

Accurate and timely reporting by the guardian ensures that the court and other governing bodies involved in the guardianship process can monitor the ward's care and ensure that their needs are being met.

Guardian reporting is a legal requirement in Florida, and failure to comply with reporting requirements can result in serious legal and financial consequences for the guardian. Non-compliance can result in fines, legal action, and even removal of the guardian.

In addition to legal compliance, guardianship reporting also ensures accountability and transparency. By providing regular reports on the ward's care, the guardian is held accountable for their actions and decisions. This helps to ensure that the guardian is acting in the best interests of the ward and that their decisions are transparent and in compliance with the law.

Lastly, guardianship reporting facilitates communication and collaboration among the various interested parties involved in the guardianship. Reports can help identify potential issues or concerns that need to be addressed and can help ensure that all parties are working together toward a common goal.

Accurate and timely reporting is essential for protecting the interests of the ward, ensuring compliance with legal and financial requirements, promoting accountability and transparency, and facilitating communication and collaboration among the various parties involved in the guardianship process.

Case Study - Ms. Bee

In 2007, I was assigned to represent Ms. Bee, a patient who had been hospitalized for over eight months. Initially, little was known about her, except that she was reported to be indigent and abandoned by her family. However, I would later discover that these claims were false.

During my visit to the hospital, it became evident that Ms. Bee was no longer sick but was unable to be discharged safely due to certain circumstances. Despite being deemed indigent by the court, hospital staff and case managers suspected that she had a pension in New York and Medicare.

When I interviewed Ms. Bee in her hospital room, I was struck by her appearance and the arrangement of her surroundings. She was adorned with pearls and had perfectly applied red lipstick. Her attire was stylish, complemented by a matching shoulder bag. Her hospital bed stands had been transformed into nightstands adorned with dolls.

To my surprise, her first words to me were, "Who are you? Are you my lawyer?" I clarified that I was her guardian, appointed by the court to assist her. She insisted on having her lawyer present and expressed her desire to have her hair and nails done, even requesting a pedicure while showing me her neglected feet. These were things Ms. Bee was accustomed to. Her hair was matted and hadn't been attended to in months. She casually mentioned, "You know I have a lot of money." I couldn't help but smile in disbelief, knowing that as a guardian, I should follow her wishes despite her capacity.

The initial phase of the inventory process began, following the requirements outlined in Statute 744[1]. It was clear from the start that, like in other cases, an inventory is more than just reporting the obvious. Guardianship requires a

---

[1] Statutes, F. (2021). "Chapter 744.365 Verified inventory." Retrieved 02/13, 2023, from https://www.flsenate.gov/Laws/Statutes/2021/Chapter744/All.

5. Governing Body & Guardianship Reporting in Florida

high level of experience to successfully account for everything during an inventory.

Since Ms. Bee was over 65 years old, she was likely entitled to Social Security benefits. However, there were no visible personal belongings or assets apart from a single suitcase of clothing and a string of pearls around her neck. Based on my observations and instincts, it seemed unlikely that she was truly indigent, and her statements held some truth. I didn't think Ms. Bee was poor.

Following the interview, I engaged in discussions with the Court Monitor, hospital staff, and Ms. Bee as part of the inventory process. I discovered that she hailed from New York City and owned an apartment near Central Park. Upon contacting the apartment complex, I learned that her rent was up to date, with automatic payments arranged through her bank. The apartment was a cooperative, and she held fractional ownership. Rent payments were being made by guests of Banko Popular Bank.

After presenting my findings, the court granted my petition and authorized a trip to New York City to assess potential assets at her apartment. This process took five days due to the extensive financial documentation and multiple meetings with the bank.

Ms. Bee's life in New York had been one of social prominence. She was well-known and well-traveled, admired by many. Her social circle consisted of influential individuals in the Latino music industry, and she had even dated a famous Latin music producer. Despite never marrying or having children, she had numerous friends. Professionally, she had served as an executive for the City of New York. Her home was modest, and her only indulgence was an expensive fur coat.

Her decline began with a stroke while she was alone at home. This was compounded by her hearing impairment, for which she wore a hearing aid. Initially, her friends attempted to help, followed by a family member and the hiring of a home health aide and caregiver. Conflicts arose between friends, caregivers, and family, making the situation unmanageable. Her memory began to deteriorate.

Subsequently, a family member brought her to Orlando, Florida, to visit and potentially stay with extended family. However, due to differences in social standards and lifestyle, this arrangement proved unsuccessful. One evening,

5. Governing Body & Guardianship Reporting in Florida

when the family went out for an event, Ms. Bee experienced a breakdown of unknown cause. She was admitted to the hospital and remained there for over seven months until I was appointed as her guardian.

In New York, I uncovered assets totaling over $650,000, including prepaid funeral arrangements, wills, cash, unclaimed funds, insurance policies, several annuities held with multiple financial institutions, and personal property. To my surprise, I also discovered that attempts at extortion had already begun, which we were able to halt.

As we transitioned Ms. Bee out of the hospital, her personal care needs became a priority. She expressed her desire for regular hair, nail, and pedicure appointments every two weeks. At 87 years old, she still reminds us when her hair is not done. Due to her medical condition, she required placement in a memory care facility. Fortunately, we were able to find a facility in central Florida that meets the National Guardianship Standard, ensuring her living conditions match the lifestyle she was accustomed to prior to her incapacity, whenever possible.

5.2. Governing Body

5.2.1. Department of Elder Affairs

The Department of Elder Affairs is a Florida State agency responsible for promoting the well-being, safety, and independence of Florida's seniors. Among its responsibilities is the oversight and regulation of the guardianship process in Florida. The governing body plays a key role in ensuring that guardians comply with reporting requirements and that the ward's interests are protected.

Regarding guardianship reporting, Florida State Statutes Chapter 744 provides information and guidance on the required reports that guardians need to submit, such as the Initial Reports, Verified Inventory, (guardian of property). Initial Plan (guardian of person), Annual Plan of the Person, and Annual Accounting of the Property.

This department is also responsible for investigating complaints and allegations of abuse or neglect related to guardianship. If the department receives a complaint or allegation, they will investigate the matter to determine whether the guardian has complied with reporting requirements and acted in the best interests of the ward.

5. Governing Body & Guardianship Reporting in Florida

More specifically, investigations may involve reviewing guardianship reports submitted by the guardian, conducting interviews with the guardian and other parties involved in the guardianship process, and conducting on-site visits to the ward's home or care facility. If the department finds evidence of abuse, neglect, or other violations, they may take legal action against the guardian, including removing the guardian. The removal process is done at the local circuit level. The Office of Professional and Public Guardians (OPPG) may deem the guardian not in compliance to serve as a guardian and may suspend their license. But the removal is a statutory sanction that is done before a judge.

5.2.2. Clerk of Court

In the State of Florida, the Clerk of Court is responsible for various administrative and judicial duties related to the guardianship process. This governing body is responsible for maintaining court records related to guardianship reports.

Initial Required Reports: Verified Inventory (guardian of property) and Initial Plan (guardian of person) Reports, Annual Plan Reports of the Person, and Annual Accounting of the Property of Guardian are submitted to The Clerk of Court. The Clerk of Court also provides guidance on how to complete and submit these reports accurately and timely. The Clerk of Court maintains court records related to guardianship reports.

Non-compliance with guardianship reporting requirements can result in legal and financial consequences for the guardian. If a guardian fails to comply with reporting requirements, the Clerk of Court may take legal action against the guardian, such as imposing fines or removing them from the guardianship role.

The Clerk of Court collaborates with other governing bodies involved in the guardianship process, such as the Department of Elder Affairs and the Probate Circuit Court. Communication and collaboration among these governing bodies are meant to ensure that guardians comply with reporting requirements.

5.2.3. Circuit_Court

In Florida, the Circuit Court has jurisdiction over the guardianship process. The court has the right to review and approve or deny guardianship reports submitted by the guardian.
This governing body can also take legal action against the guardian if they fail to comply with reporting requirements or if there is evidence of abuse or neglect.

5.3. Guardianship Reporting in Florida

5.3.1. Reports – Plan and Inventory

In the state of Florida, Initial Reports are due 60 days after the Letters are signed appointing the guardian: a Verified Inventory by the guardian of property and The Initial Plan by the guardian of the person. The purpose of these reports is to provide an inventory of the ward's assets and liabilities, as well as a plan for their care and management.

The Verified Inventory provides information on the ward's assets and liabilities on the date of the Letter of Guardianship (LOG). The Initial Report of Guardian of the Person outlines the guardian's plan for the ward's care and management.

The Verified Inventory and Initial Plan Report of Guardian must be filed with the circuit court of the venue of the guardianship. The report must be filed within 60 days of the guardian's appointment LOG.

More specifically, the Verified Inventory Initial Report must include the following information:

Detailed inventory of assets:

- A list of the ward's assets, including both tangible and intangible assets.
- Tangible assets may include real estate properties, vehicles, jewelry, artwork, and personal belongings.
- Intangible assets may consist of financial accounts, investments, stocks, bonds, and other monetary holdings.

Description and identification of each asset:

- Specific details about each asset, such as make, model, serial numbers, or any unique identifiers.
- The report should contain a clear description that helps identify and differentiate the assets listed in the inventory.

Accurate valuation of assets:

- Value to each asset will be assigned based on its current market worth or fair market value at the time of reporting.
- Guardians need to consider obtaining appraisals when necessary.

5. Governing Body & Guardianship Reporting in Florida

Liabilities and debts:

- Includes outstanding debts, mortgages, loans, or other financial obligations associated with the ward's assets.
- Includes information about creditors, amounts owed, and repayment terms, if applicable.

The Initial Plan Report of Guardian of property is a legal document that must be filed by a guardian in Florida when they are appointed to manage the affairs of a ward. The Initial Plan Report of Guardian of Person outlines the guardian's plan for the ward's care and management, and it serves as a roadmap for the guardian's activities for the upcoming year.

The Initial Plan Report of the Guardian of Person has the following requirements:

1. **Identification of the ward and the guardian:** The report should contain the ward's name, date of birth, and address, as well as the guardian's name and contact information.

   Statement of the ward's capacity: The document should include a statement on the ward's capacity, indicating whether they are completely or partially incapacitated, and explaining the reasons for their incapacity.

Statement of the guardian's qualifications: The file must include a statement of the guardian's qualifications, explaining why they are suitable to serve as the ward's guardian.

Plan for the ward's care and management: The report must contain a plan for the ward's care and management, outlining the guardian's strategy for meeting the ward's needs and ensuring their well-being. The plan should include information on the ward's medical and personal care needs, as well as any special needs or preferences they may have.

After the Initial Report of Guardian, the guardian is required to file an Annual Plan Report of the Guardian. This is a report that the guardian of person must file every year to provide information on the ward's well-being, living conditions, and any changes in their personal circumstances.

The Annual Plan Report of the Guardian must be filed 90-days after the last day of the anniversary month that the Letters were signed. Failure

5. Governing Body & Guardianship Reporting in Florida

to file this report on time can result in legal and financial consequences for the guardian, including fines or removal as the guardian. The report must be filed with the Probate Division of the Circuit Court in the county of jurisdiction.

More specifically, the Annual Plan Report of the Guardian of Person must include the following information:

1. **Identification of the ward and the guardian:** The report should include the ward's name, address, as well as the guardian's name and contact information.

2. **Information on the ward's well-being and living conditions:** The document should include information on the ward's physical and mental health, as well as their living conditions. This may include information on any medical treatments or procedures, medications, or changes in their living environment.

3. **Changes in the ward's personal circumstances:** The file should include information on any changes in the ward's personal circumstances, such as changes in their family or social

relationships, or changes in their financial situation.

4. **Guardian's activities during the reporting period:** The report should include information on the guardian's activities during the reporting period, including any decisions made on behalf of the ward, any expenses incurred, and any issues or concerns that arose during the reporting period.

5. **A statement of an existing Do Not Resuscitate (DNR) or other pre-need arrangements.**

6. **Actions being taken to take care of the ward's social and emotional needs.**

7. **Residential history.**

8. **Hospitalizations and medical history.**

9. **Plan for medical care:** Name and addresses of medical care providers, insurance providers and other treatment providers.

10. **A summary of the care goals for the period, year covered by the plan.**

5. Governing Body & Guardianship Reporting in Florida

A guardian in Florida is also required to file an Annual Accounting of Guardian by the guardian of property. This document provides information on the ward's financial affairs and the guardian's management of their assets.

The Annual Accounting of Guardian must be filed 90-days after the last day of the anniversary month the Letters were signed. The document is filed with the Probate Division of the Circuit Court in the county of the jurisdiction of the guardianship.

The Annual Accounting Report of Guardian must include the following information:

1. A full and correct account of the receipts and disbursements of all the ward's property over which the guardian has control and a statement of the ward's property in hand at the end of the accounting period. (This does not apply to any property or any trust of which the ward is a beneficiary, but which is not under the control or administration of the guardian).

2. A copy of the annual or year-end statement of all the ward's cash accounts from each of the institutions where the cash is deposited.

3. A report of all real and personal property owned by the Ward and under the control of the guardian.

4. The guardian must obtain a receipt, canceled check, or other proof of payment for all expenditures and disbursements made on behalf of the ward. The guardian must preserve all evidence of payment, along with other substantiating papers, for a period of 3 years after his or her discharge. The receipts, proofs of payment, and substantiating papers need not be filed with the court but shall be made available for inspection and review at the time and place and before the persons as the court may order.

5. The guardian shall pay from the ward's estate to the Clerk of the Circuit Court a fee based upon the following graduated fee schedule, upon the filing of the annual financial return, for the auditing of the return:

   - For estates with a value of $25,000 or less the clerk of the court may charge a fee of up to $20, from which the clerk shall remit $5 to the Department of Revenue for deposit into the General Revenue Fund.

- For estates with a value of more than $25,000 up to and including $100,000 the clerk of the court may charge a fee of up to $85, from which the clerk shall remit $10 to the Department of Revenue for deposit into the General Revenue Funds.

- For estates with a value of more than $100,000 up to and including $500,000 the clerk of the court may charge a fee of up to $170, from which the clerk shall remit $20 to the Department of Revenue for deposit into the General Revenue Fund.

- For estates with a value in excess of $500,000 the clerk of the court may charge a fee of up to $250, from which the clerk shall remit $25 to the Department of Revenue for deposit into the General Revenue Fund.

Upon petition by the guardian, the court may waive the auditing fee upon a showing of insufficient funds in the ward's estate. Any guardian unable to pay the auditing fee may petition the court for a waiver of the fee. The court may waive the fee after it has reviewed the documentation filed by the guardian in support of the waiver.

This does not apply if the court determines that the ward's only income is from Social Security benefits and the guardian is the ward's representative payee for the benefits. In such cases the guardian may petition the court to waive annual accounting reports.

5.3.2 Understanding Reporting periods

At first, reporting periods may seem simple. You get assigned a case and the reports are annual. Well, true and not-so-true. While the statues may say 'annually', the actual reporting periods are far from that simple.

Even though you are allowed to petition the court for extensions, initial reports are due 60 days after the Letters of Guardianship are signed by the judge.

In a case where an Emergency Temporary Guardianship (ETG) was made, The ETG authority lasts for 90-days or until the permanent guardian is appointed, with one additional 90-day extension. Reporting is not required during this period, however, during this time you must maintain the

5. Governing Body & Guardianship Reporting in Florida

full responsibilities of guardianship and keep adequate records.

If you are appointed the permanent guardian, following an Emergency Temporary Guardianship your Initial Guardianship Report reporting period starts from the original date of the ETG and ends the following year on the last day of the month indicated on the Letter of Guardianship. This, in most cases, will be more than twelve months.

If you are an ETG and are not appointed the permanent guardian, your final report is due 30 days after the permanent guardian is appointed. If you are appointed the permanent guardian, the same reporting times apply for the Initial Reports.

This can best be explained by an example. For our example:

- ETG was January 15, 2023.
- The Letter of Guardianship (LOG) is March 10, 2023
- And you are appointed plenary guardian (guardian of person and property).

The reporting dates in this example are:

- The Verified Inventory Report of Guardian will have a report date of January 15, 2023. The date of the ETG.

- The following year (2024), the Annual Accounting Report of Guardian is required and will cover the period of January 15, 2023 through March 31, 2024 (the end of the month that the LOG was signed). It is key to remember that accounting is for the previous 12 months.

- The Initial Report of Guardian will have the date of January 15, 2023, the date of the ETG, and run through March 31, 2024.

- Thereafter, Annual Plans are due and run from April 1, 2024, through March 31, 2025. It is key to remember that the Annual Plans cover the plan of care for the next twelve months.

This also applies to Guardian Advocate if you were appointed guardian advocate for Developmentally Delayed Person instead of Guardian of Person.

5. Governing Body & Guardianship Reporting in Florida

In appointments where you are directly appointed Guardian of Person and you were not Emergency Temporary Guardian reporting starts on the date of the Letter of Guardianship. The initial plan would be dated March 10, 2023 to March 31, 2024.

Thereafter Annual Plans reporting would begin on April 1, the next year and end the last day of the preceding month.

The message here is, make sure you understand the reporting periods. I have given only one example, but there can be other situations as well.

5.3.3. Record Keeping and Case Notes

Guardians are required to maintain records and case notes to document their activities and decisions on behalf of the ward. These records can be used to support the Annual Reports of the Person and Annual Accounting of Guardian and can be helpful in resolving disputes or addressing issues that may arise during the guardianship process.

These records should include documentation of all transactions involving the ward's assets, including deposits, withdrawals, and transfers. Guardians should also keep records of any expenses incurred on behalf of the ward, such as medical bills or other costs related to their care.

In addition to financial records, guardians must maintain records of all communication with the ward, including phone calls, emails, and in-person conversations. These records can be helpful in demonstrating the guardian's compliance with reporting requirements.

Case notes are detailed records of the guardian's activities and decisions on behalf of the ward. These notes must include information on any decisions made by the guardian, such as medical treatments or financial transactions, as well as any issues or concerns that arise during the guardianship process.

Case notes should be detailed and thorough, providing a clear record of the guardian's activities and decisions. They should be organized and easy to understand so that they can be used to support the Annual Reports of the Person and Annual Accounting of the Guardian, as well as any legal proceedings that may arise during the guardianship process.

5.4. Chapter Summary

This chapter provided an overview of the different governing bodies involved in the guardianship process and the process of guardianship reporting in Florida.

5. Governing Body & Guardianship Reporting in Florida

You now know that there are three main bodies that govern guardianship in the state. Understanding the purpose of each of them in relation to guardianship reporting can be useful for both guardians and those working with them.

- **The Department of Elder Affairs** in Florida is responsible for promoting the well-being, safety, and independence of seniors, including overseeing, and regulating the guardianship process.

The Clerk of Court in Florida has administrative and judicial duties in the guardianship process, including maintaining court records related to guardianship reports.

- **The Probate Circuit Court** in Florida is responsible for appointing guardians and overseeing the guardianship process.

- **The Verified Inventory** and **Initial Report of Guardian** are the first reports that a guardian must file in a guardianship case, providing an inventory of the ward's assets and liabilities, as well as a plan for their care and management.

- provides information on the ward's well-being, living conditions, and any changes in their personal circumstances.

- **Annual Accounting of Guardian** provides information on the ward's financial affairs and the guardian's management of their assets.

Understanding the relationship between the Department of Elder Affairs, the Clerk of Court, and the Probate Circuit Court is important for guardians in Florida as they navigate the guardianship process. These governing bodies work together to regulate and oversee the guardianship process, ensuring that guardians comply with reporting requirements.

It is equally important to understand the requirements for the Verified Inventory Initial Report, Annual Report of the Person, and Annual Accounting of Guardian, as well as to know how to submit them accurately and timely. By doing so, guardians can avoid legal and financial consequences, including fines or removal from the guardianship role.

By following the guidance and information provided in this chapter, I believe that guardians will have an easier time carrying out their responsibilities effectively, ensuring that the guardianship process runs smoothly, protecting the interests of the ward, and maintaining transparency and accountability throughout the process.

6. Determining When Guardianship is Needed

6.1. Overview

Determining whether guardianship is necessary involves evaluating the capacity of an individual to make decisions related to their personal and financial affairs.

Guardianship may be necessary in cases where an individual is unable to make decisions due to a mental or physical disability. The court will appoint a guardian to make decisions on behalf of the individual if they are deemed incapacitated.

In this chapter, I will discuss the criteria for determining incapacity, the guardian's family needs, issues, and processes. In addition, I will also provide a review of alternatives to guardianship, such as durable power of attorney and healthcare surrogate designation.

First, I will introduce readers to the process of guardianship for persons with substance abuse and other mental disorders. In Florida, there are two laws that provide for the involuntary assessment and treatment of individuals with substance abuse and mental health disorders: the Baker Act and the Marchman Act.

I will provide a detailed explanation of the Baker Act, a law that provides for the involuntary examination and treatment of individuals with mental health disorders who are unable to make decisions for themselves. The act allows for the temporary detention of up to 72 hours for evaluation and stabilization of the individual.

The Marchman Act, on the other hand, provides for the involuntary assessment and treatment of individuals with substance abuse disorders who are unable to make decisions for themselves. The act allows for a temporary detention of up to 5 days for the assessment and stabilization of the individual.

The second topic of this chapter concerns the needs, issues, and processes that family guardians must be aware of. As discussed elsewhere, a family member or other interested person may petition the court to become a guardian of an individual who is incapacitated.

6. Determining When Guardianship is Needed

The process of becoming a guardian involves an evaluation of the proposed guardian's qualifications and a determination of the individual's incapacity. There are several issues that may arise during the guardianship process, including conflicts among family members and disagreements about the care and treatment of the incapacitated individual.

Finally, the last section will explain why, in some cases, alternatives to guardianship may be appropriate. Some of the alternatives include having:

- Advance directives
- Health care surrogate decision-making
- Assistance with personal needs
- Durable Power of Attorney
- Representative payees
- Banking services
- ABLE accounts
- Trusts
- Voluntary Guardian of Property

Durable Power of Attorney

A durable power of attorney is a legal document that allows an individual to appoint someone to make decisions on their behalf if they become incapacitated. This document can be used to designate someone to make financial and legal decisions.

Healthcare Surrogate

A healthcare surrogate designation is a legal document. It allows an individual to appoint someone to make healthcare decisions on their behalf if they become incapacitated, usually due to hospitalization or sickness. The designee can make decisions related to medical treatment and end-of-life care.

6.2. Guardianship for Persons with Substance Abuse and Other Mental Disorders

6.2.1 Baker Act

The Baker Act[2] is a Florida law that provides for the involuntary examination and treatment of individuals with mental health disorders who are unable to make decisions for themselves.

The law is named after Maxine Baker, a former state representative who advocated for mental

---

[2] Statutes, F. (2023). "Florida Statutes, Chapter CCCXCIV, Section 394.451." Retrieved 03/07, 2023, from http://www.leg.state.fl.us/statutes/index.cfm?App_mode=Display_Statute&Search_String=&URL=0700-0799/0744/Sections/0744.331.html.

6. Determining When Guardianship is Needed

health services. The purpose of the Baker Act is to protect individuals with mental health disorders and provide them with necessary treatment and care.

The Baker Act has become an increasingly important tool for addressing mental health issues in Florida, particularly with the rise of substance abuse and mental health disorders in the state. The law is designed to provide a pathway for individuals who are unable to make decisions for themselves due to mental illness to receive the treatment they need.

To initiate the Baker Act process, an individual must meet specific criteria for involuntary examination, including having a mental illness, being a danger to themselves or others, and being unable to make decisions for themselves.

Mental Illness

One of the primary criteria for involuntary examination under the Baker Act is that the individual must have a mental illness.

In this context, mental illness is understood to be an impairment of the mental or emotional processes that exercise conscious control of one's actions or of the ability to perceive or understand reality. This definition is intentionally broad to ensure that individuals who may be suffering from a wide range of conditions are able to receive the necessary care and treatment they need.[3]

Schizophrenia, bipolar disorder, and major depression are a few examples of mental illnesses or conditions that may meet the criteria for involuntary examination under the Baker Act.

Danger to Themselves or Others

Another criterion for involuntary examination under the Baker Act is that the individual must be a danger to themselves or others. This criterion is designed to ensure that individuals who pose a risk to themselves or others due to their mental illness are evaluated and provided with the necessary treatment and care. In this context, a dangerous person is someone who is likely to cause harm to themselves or others.[4]

There are several behaviors that may indicate that an individual is a danger to themselves or others and may meet the criteria for involuntary

---

[3] Families, F. D. o. C. a. "Baker Act." Retrieved 21/03, 2023, from https://www.myflfamilies.com/crisis-services/baker-act.

[4] Alcohol, D. A. (1989). "Mental Health Program Office: Annual report to the Florida Legislature." <u>Florida Department of Health and Rehabilitative Services</u>.

examination under the Baker Act. These include suicidal statements or attempts, threats of harm to others, and engaging in violent or aggressive behavior.

Inability to Make Decisions

The third criterion for involuntary examination under the Baker Act is that the individual is unable to make decisions for themselves. This criterion is designed to ensure that individuals who are not able to make decisions related to their personal or financial affairs due to their mental illness are evaluated and provided with the necessary treatment and care.

A person who is unable to make decisions for themselves is said to be incapacitated. An incapacitated person is someone who has a physical or mental condition that prevents them from making decisions related to their personal or financial affairs.[5]

Once an individual has been involuntarily admitted for examination under the Baker Act,

---

[5] Statutes, F. (2023). Florida Statutes, Chapter DCCXLIV, Section 744.102(12)Retrieved 03/07, 2023, from http://www.leg.state.fl.us/statutes/index.cfm?App_mode=Display_Statute&Search_String=&URL=0700-0799/0744/Sections/0744.331.html.

they will undergo an evaluation period to determine their mental health status and any potential risks they may pose to themselves or others.

This evaluation period typically lasts up to 72 hours, during which time the individual will be examined by qualified mental health professionals to determine their mental health status and any necessary treatment options.

The evaluation of the individual during the 72-hour period is designed to be thorough and objective. The evaluation includes a review of the individual's medical history, an examination of their current mental state, and an assessment of any potential risks they may pose to themselves or others.

During the evaluation period, the individual will receive treatments such as counseling or therapy, and may be given medications to stabilize the individual's mental health so that they can be safely discharged from the hospital or transferred to a more appropriate treatment facility.

There are several treatment options available to individuals who are admitted under the Baker Act for involuntary examination. These treatment options include:

6. Determining When Guardianship is Needed

- **Outpatient Treatment:** This treatment option involves ongoing therapy and medication management on an outpatient basis. Individuals who are deemed stable enough to be discharged from the hospital may be referred to an outpatient mental health facility for ongoing treatment.

- **Inpatient Treatment:** This treatment option involves hospitalization for individuals who require more intensive treatment and care. Inpatient treatment may be necessary for individuals who pose a significant risk to themselves or others, or who require more intensive therapy and medication management.

- **Partial Hospitalization:** This treatment option involves a structured treatment program that combines elements of both inpatient and outpatient treatment. Individuals who participate in partial hospitalization typically attend therapy and other treatment programs during the day and return home in the evening.

To be released from involuntary examination, the individual must meet certain criteria, including:

1. The individual is no longer a danger to themselves or others;

2. The individual is able to make decisions for themselves;

3. The individual has a treatment plan in place to address their mental health needs.

If the individual is not able to be safely released from involuntary examination, they may be transferred to a more appropriate treatment facility for further care and treatment.

Individuals who are admitted under the Baker Act for the involuntary examination have certain legal rights that are designed to protect them during the evaluation and treatment process.

These rights include:

1. The right to be informed of their rights and the nature of the evaluation and treatment process;

2. The right to receive visitors and communicate with family members and legal representatives;

3. The right to refuse treatment, except in certain circumstances where treatment is

6. Determining When Guardianship is Needed

necessary to prevent harm to themselves or others.[6]

After the involuntary examination period has ended, individuals who are admitted under the Baker Act have certain legal rights related to their care and treatment, including:

1. The right to be informed of their treatment options (including outpatient treatment, inpatient treatment, and partial hospitalization);

2. The right to participate in decisions related to their care and treatment; and

3. The right to receive appropriate care and treatment (this may include medication management, therapy, and other forms of treatment).

If an individual or their legal representative disagrees with the involuntary examination and treatment process under the Baker Act, they may contest the decision through a legal process. This process involves filing a petition for habeas corpus, which is a legal proceeding that allows an individual to challenge their detention or imprisonment.

---

[6] LHRM, C. (2008). "Baker Act Basics."

The process for contesting the Baker Act can be complex, and individuals who are considering challenging their detention should consult with an attorney who is experienced in mental health law. An attorney can provide guidance and support throughout the legal process and help individuals navigate the complex legal system.

The Baker Act process can be initiated by anyone: an individual, medical institution, or a residential living facility such as an assisted or independent living facility. However, it is most often done by law enforcement.

6.2.2. Marchman Act

The Marchman Act[7] is a law in the state of Florida that allows individuals to be involuntarily assessed and stabilized for substance abuse disorders.

The purpose of the Marchman Act is to provide individuals who are struggling with substance abuse disorders with the necessary care and treatment they need to address their condition.

---

[7] Statutes, F. (2023). Florida Statutes, Chapter CCCXCVII Retrieved 03/07, 2023, from http://www.leg.state.fl.us/statutes/index.cfm?App_mode=Display_Statute&Search_String=&URL=0700-0799/0744/Sections/0744.331.html.

6. Determining When Guardianship is Needed

The Marchman Act can be initiated by a concerned family member, healthcare professional, or law enforcement officer who believes that an individual is abusing drugs or alcohol and is a danger to themselves or others.

Once the Marchman Act is initiated, the individual will undergo a comprehensive assessment and stabilization period to determine their substance abuse status and any potential risks they may pose to themselves or others.

The criteria for involuntary assessment and stabilization under the Marchman Act are designed to identify individuals who are in need of immediate intervention for substance abuse disorders. The criteria include the following:

1. The individual has lost the power of self-control with respect to substance abuse and is likely to cause harm to themselves or others if not admitted for assessment and stabilization.

    This criterion is intended to identify individuals who are unable to control their substance abuse and who may pose a danger to themselves or others. This may include individuals who have a history of drug or alcohol-related accidents or injuries, or who have engaged in other risky behaviors as a result of their substance abuse.

2. The individual has refused to voluntarily seek assessment and stabilization for their substance abuse disorder.

   This criterion is meant to identify individuals who are in denial about their substance abuse disorder and who are not willing to seek help voluntarily. In some cases, individuals may be unable to recognize the severity of their substance abuse disorder or may be resistant to the idea of seeking treatment.

3. The individual is unable to recognize the need for assessment and stabilization due to their substance abuse disorder.

   This criterion is intended to identify individuals who are unable to recognize the severity of their substance abuse disorder due to the effects of drugs or alcohol. This may include individuals who are in a state of delirium or who are experiencing other mental health symptoms as a result of their substance abuse.

There are a variety of behaviors that may meet the criteria for involuntary assessment and

6. Determining When Guardianship is Needed

stabilization under the Marchman Act. These behaviors may include:

- A history of multiple drug overdoses
- Repeated instances of driving under the influence of drugs or alcohol
- A pattern of drug or alcohol abuse that has resulted in legal or financial problems
- A pattern of erratic or violent behavior that is directly related to substance abuse

The specific behaviors that meet the criteria for involuntary assessment and stabilization may vary depending on the individual's substance abuse history, as well as their physical and mental health status.

The process for initiating involuntary assessment and stabilization under the Marchman Act typically involves several steps, including:

Petition for assessment and stabilization

The process begins when a family member, healthcare professional, or law enforcement officer files a petition for assessment and stabilization with the court. The petition must provide evidence that the individual is in need of immediate intervention for substance abuse disorders.

Court hearing

After the petition is filed, the court will schedule a hearing to determine whether the individual meets the criteria for involuntary assessment and stabilization under the Marchman Act. The individual has the right to be represented by an attorney at the hearing.

Assessment and stabilization

If the court determines that the individual meets the criteria for involuntary assessment and stabilization, they will be admitted to a licensed assessment and stabilization facility for evaluation and treatment. The assessment and stabilization period is typically 5 days, but it may be extended for up to 10 days if necessary.

Criteria for release or further treatment

The individual must meet certain criteria for release or further treatment before they can be discharged from the assessment and stabilization facility.

The process of involuntary assessment and stabilization under the Marchman Act is meant to be fast and efficient so that individuals who are in need of immediate intervention for substance abuse disorders can receive the necessary care and treatment as soon as possible.

The process involves several steps, including initiation of the process, court hearing, assessment

6. Determining When Guardianship is Needed

and stabilization, and criteria for release or further treatment.

The timeline for the process of involuntary assessment typically follows the following steps:

- Within 24 hours of filing the petition, the court will schedule a hearing to determine whether the individual meets the criteria for involuntary assessment and stabilization.
- Within 72 hours of the court's determination, the individual will be admitted to a licensed assessment and stabilization facility for evaluation and treatment.

Individuals who are involuntarily admitted for assessment and stabilization under the Marchman Act have certain legal rights that are designed to protect them during the process. These rights include:

- The right to legal representation at the court hearing.
- The right to receive treatment and counseling during the assessment and stabilization period.
- The right to refuse treatment, unless a court has determined that they meet the criteria for involuntary assessment and stabilization.

Individuals who believe that they have been involuntarily admitted for assessment and stabilization under the Marchman Act without sufficient cause may contest the process by filing a petition for habeas corpus. A petition for habeas corpus is a legal action that allows individuals to challenge their detention in court.[8]

The following treatment options may be available during the assessment and stabilization period:

Detoxification

Detoxification is the process of removing drugs or alcohol from the body. This may be necessary for individuals who are physically dependent on drugs or alcohol and who may experience withdrawal symptoms when they stop using.

Medication-Assisted Treatment

Medication-assisted treatment is a form of treatment that uses medication to manage withdrawal symptoms and reduce cravings for drugs or alcohol.

Counseling

Counseling is an important component of substance abuse treatment. Counseling may include

---

[8] Oaks, D. H. (1966). "Legal History in the High Court: Habeas Corpus." Michigan Law Review **64**(3): 451-472.

6. Determining When Guardianship is Needed

individual therapy, group therapy, or family therapy, and it may be provided by licensed healthcare professionals who specialize in substance abuse treatment.

Individuals must meet certain criteria for release or further treatment. These criteria may include:

1. *Completion* of an initial treatment plan Individuals must complete an initial treatment plan that is developed during the assessment and stabilization period.

2. *Participation* in ongoing treatment and counseling: Individuals must participate in ongoing treatment and counseling to address their substance abuse disorder.

3. *Adherence* to any court-ordered conditions: Individuals must adhere to any court-ordered conditions that are designed to ensure their safety and prevent further harm to themselves or others.

Individuals who are admitted for assessment and stabilization under the Marchman Act have certain legal rights that are designed to protect them during the process. These rights include the right to receive treatment and counseling during the assessment and stabilization period, the right to refuse treatment unless a court has determined that they meet the criteria for involuntary assessment and stabilization, and the right to legal representation at the court hearing. Let's take a closer look at each of these rights.

4. *Right to Legal Representation.* Individuals have the right to be represented by an attorney at the court hearing that determines whether they meet the criteria for involuntary assessment and stabilization. This allows individuals to have legal representation and protect their rights during the process.

5. *Right to Receive Treatment and Counseling.* Those admitted for assessment and stabilization under the Marchman Act have the right to receive treatment and counseling during the assessment and stabilization period. This ensures that individuals receive the necessary care and treatment they need to address their substance abuse disorder and prevent further harm to themselves or others.

6. *Right to Refuse Treatment.* Individuals who are admitted for assessment and stabilization under the Marchman Act have the right to refuse treatment unless a court has determined that they meet the

criteria for involuntary assessment and stabilization.

Finally, while the Marchman Act provides a legal framework for assessment and stabilization, it may not provide adequate support for ongoing treatment and counseling. Lack of follow-up can lead to relapse and a lack of sustained recovery.

6.3. Alternatives to Guardianship

6.3.1. Durable Power of Attorney

A durable power of attorney (DPOA) is an important legal tool that allows an individual (the principal) to appoint another person (the agent or attorney-in-fact) to make decisions on their behalf in the event that they become incapacitated or unable to make decisions. In Florida, a durable power of attorney is governed by Chapter 709 of the Florida Statutes.[9]

A DPOA can provide peace of mind knowing that important decisions can be made on your behalf by someone you trust, if you are unable to make

---

[9] Statutes, F. (2023). Florida Statutes, Chapter VII IX Retrieved 03/07, 2023, from http://www.leg.state.fl.us/statutes/index.cfm?App_mode=Display_Statute&Search_String=&URL=0700-0799/0744/Sections/0744.331.html.

them yourself, who can make important decisions regarding your financial affairs, health care, and other matters that could otherwise be handled by a guardian.[10]

A durable power of attorney is different from a regular power of attorney in that it remains in effect even if the principal becomes incapacitated or unable to make decisions. In contrast, a regular power of attorney typically becomes invalid if the principal becomes incapacitated. This is what makes a DPOA an important estate planning tool.

There are several reasons why someone may choose to create a durable power of attorney. For example, a DPOA can be used to:

1. *Ensure that important decisions are made by someone the principal trusts* - A durable power of attorney allows the principal to appoint an agent who will make important decisions on their behalf if they become incapacitated. By appointing someone they trust, the principal can ensure that their wishes are carried out in the event of incapacity.

---

[10] Desai, A. and A. O. Giwa (2019). "Power of Attorney."

6. Determining When Guardianship is Needed

2. *Provide flexibility and control* - A DPOA can be customized to meet the principal's specific needs and wishes. The principal can choose the agent, specify the scope of the agent's authority, and include any conditions or limitations they wish to impose. This provides the principal with flexibility and control over the decision-making process.

Note that a durable power of attorney only remains in effect while the principal is alive. Once the principal dies, the DPOA becomes invalid, and any decisions must be made by the executor of the principal's estate or by a court-appointed administrator.

Choosing a DPOA is an important decision that should not be taken lightly. The person chosen to be the agent or attorney-in-fact will be responsible for making important decisions on behalf of the principal if they become incapacitated. Therefore, you will want to choose someone who is trustworthy, responsible, and capable of carrying out the duties of the role.

There are several factors to consider when choosing a durable power of attorney. For instance, the agent chosen as the DPOA should be someone the principal trusts implicitly.

The agent will be responsible and capable of managing the principal's affairs. This includes financial affairs, legal matters, and health care decisions. As such, the agent should be someone who has experience managing their own affairs and is able to make sound decisions on behalf of the principal.

In addition, the agent should be available to act as the DPOA if and when the time comes. This means that they should be reachable and able to respond quickly if called upon to make decisions on the principal's behalf.

It is also important that the agent is someone who is able to communicate effectively with the principal and with other family members or individuals involved in the decision-making process. This includes being able to provide regular updates and being open to feedback and input from others.

Last but not least, there are certain legal requirements that must be met when choosing a durable power of attorney. For example, the agent must be at least 18 years old and not have a felony conviction. *Additionally, the principal must be of sound mind and capable of understanding the nature and consequences of the DPOA.*

When choosing a durable power of attorney, it is important to discuss the decision with the

6. Determining When Guardianship is Needed

potential agent before making it official. This allows the agent to understand the responsibilities involved and ensures that they are willing and able to take on the role. It also provides an opportunity for the principal to discuss their wishes and expectations with the agent, which can help to avoid misunderstandings or conflicts down the road.

It is also important to name alternate agents in the DPOA document in case the primary agent is unable or unwilling to act. This ensures that there is someone else who can step in if needed.

Creating a DPOA is a straightforward process. The first step is to choose an agent, also known as an attorney-in-fact. The agent will be responsible for making decisions on behalf of the principal if they become incapacitated.

Once an agent has been selected, the next step is to determine the powers that will be granted to the agent. This can include managing the principal's financial affairs, making health care decisions, managing legal matters, and more. The powers granted can be broad or narrow depending on the principal's wishes. The principal should consider what decisions they would want the agent to make on their behalf if they were unable to do so themselves.

The next step is to draft the DPOA document. This can be done with the assistance of an attorney or by using a template or form provided by the state. It is important to ensure that the document complies with state laws and includes all necessary information. The document should clearly state the agent's powers and limitations, the principal's wishes, and any conditions or restrictions placed on the agent's authority.

Once the document has been drafted, it must be signed and executed according to state laws. This typically involves signing the document in the presence of witnesses or a notary public. You will want to ensure that the document is executed properly to avoid any issues in the future.

When utilizing a DPOA, there are several best practices that should be followed to ensure that the document is used properly and serves its intended purpose. These include:

1. *Keeping the document current* - It is important to review and update the DPOA periodically to ensure that it remains current and reflects the principal's wishes. If circumstances change, such as the agent becoming unavailable or unsuitable to act, the document should be updated to reflect these changes.

6. Determining When Guardianship is Needed

2. *Providinc Copies to relevant parties* - It is necessary to provide copies of the DPOA to relevant parties, such as financial institutions, healthcare providers, and attorneys so that they are aware of the agent's authority and can properly recognize and act on the document.

3. *Communicating with the agent* - The principal should communicate regularly with the agent and provide guidance on their wishes and preferences. This can help avoid misunderstandings or misinterpretations of the principal's wishes.

4. *Ensuring proper execution* - The DPOA needs to be executed properly and in compliance with state laws. This can help avoid any challenges to the validity of the document in the future.

5. *Limiting the agent's authority* - The principal may choose to limit the agent's authority to specific tasks or areas of decision-making. This can help ensure that the agent is acting within the principal's wishes and avoid any abuse or misuse of the agent's authority.

6.3.2. Designation of Heath Care Surrogate

A Designation of Health Care Surrogate is a legal document that allows an individual to appoint a surrogate to make health care decisions on their behalf if they become incapacitated or unable to make decisions for themselves. In the state of Florida, a Designation of Health Care Surrogate is an important legal tool that can help ensure that an individual's medical wishes are respected and carried out in the event of an unexpected medical emergency.[11]

There are several key aspects to consider when thinking about a Designation of Health Care Surrogate. These include understanding the legal requirements for creating the document, identifying a suitable surrogate, and discussing medical wishes and preferences with the surrogate.

In Florida, a Designation of Health Care Surrogate must meet certain legal requirements to be considered valid. According to Chapter 765 of the Florida Statutes, a Designation of Health

---

[11] Statutes, F. (2023). Florida Statutes, Chapter DC LXV Retrieved 03/07, 2023, from
http://www.leg.state.fl.us/statutes/index.cfm?App_mode=Display_Statute&Search_String=&URL=0700-0799/0744/Sections/0744.331.html.

6. Determining When Guardianship is Needed

Care Surrogate must be in writing and signed by the individual making the designation, or by another person in their presence and at their direction. The document must also be signed by two witnesses, neither of whom can be the designated surrogate, and it must be dated.

In addition to these basic requirements, a Designation of Health Care Surrogate can also include specific instructions or limitations on the surrogate's authority, as well as any preferences or values that the individual wants the surrogate to consider when making medical decisions.

It's best practice to consult with an attorney or other qualified professional when creating a Designation of Healthcare Surrogate to ensure that all legal requirements are met and that the document accurately reflects the individual's wishes and preferences.

Once a suitable surrogate has been identified, it is recommended to have a thorough discussion about the individual's medical wishes and preferences. This can include discussing end-of-life care options, such as resuscitation and life support, as well as any specific medical conditions or treatments that the individual may want or not want.

It is important to be clear and specific about medical wishes and preferences and to document these preferences in the Designation of Health Care Surrogate form. This can help ensure that the surrogate has a clear understanding of the individual's wishes and can make informed decisions in accordance with those wishes.

In general, the following steps are required to create a legally binding Designation of Health Care Surrogate:

1. *Choose a health care surrogate* - The first step in creating a healthcare surrogate designation is to choose a surrogate who will be responsible for making medical decisions on your behalf if you are unable to do so.

2. *Complete a Designation of Health Care Surrogate form* - In Florida, the Designation of Health Care Surrogate form is available from a variety of sources, including hospitals, nursing homes, and health care providers. This form is also available from the Florida Department of Health website. The form is typically short and easy to complete, and it requires the following information:

6. Determining When Guardianship is Needed

- The name, address, and phone number of the person you are designating as your surrogate.
- The name, address, and phone number of an alternate surrogate in case your first choice is unavailable.
- Your signature and the date you signed the form.

3. *Sign and date the form* - Once you have completed the Designation of Health Care Surrogate form, you must sign and date it in the presence of two witnesses. The witnesses must be adults who are *not* related to you or to the person you are designating as your surrogate. They must also sign the form in your presence.

4. *Notify your surrogate* - *After* you have completed the form and had it witnessed, it is important to notify your surrogate of your decision. Discuss your wishes for medical treatment and end-of-life care with your surrogate, and make sure they understand your wishes.

5. *Store the form* - Once the form has been completed and signed, you will want to keep it in a safe place where it can be easily accessed if needed. You should also provide a copy to your surrogate, your

doctor, and any other relevant healthcare providers.

Note that a healthcare surrogate designation only becomes effective when you are unable to make your own medical decisions. Until that time, you retain the right to make your own medical decisions and can revoke or change your designation at any time.

It is recommended to periodically review and update your health care surrogate designation to ensure that it accurately reflects your wishes and that your designated surrogate is still willing and able to serve in this capacity.

It's worth noting that your surrogate may need to access your medical records to make informed decisions about your care. In Florida, a healthcare surrogate has the right to access your medical records and to share them with healthcare providers as necessary.

Finally, in some cases, there may be disagreements between family members or health care providers about medical decisions. Florida law provides a process for resolving these disputes through the courts. If a dispute arises, your surrogate should seek legal advice and guidance to help resolve the issue.

6.4. Chapter Summary

I believe that this chapter has provided valuable insights into the legal and practical considerations that must be taken into account when making decisions about guardianship. The chapter has covered a range of topics including the criteria for involuntary examination under the Baker Act and Marchman Act, the role of family guardians, and the alternatives to guardianship such as Durable Power of Attorney and Designation of Health Care Surrogate.

While both the Baker Act and Marchman Act are not always considered as part of guardianship, they deal with the care of persons with incapacity. That is what guardianship is all about. They are valuable tools for providing care.

As shown, the Baker Act and Marchman Act provide a legal framework for individuals who are struggling with mental health or substance abuse disorders. These acts allow individuals to receive the necessary evaluation and treatment they need, even if they are unable or unwilling to seek help on their own.

It is important to understand the criteria for involuntary examination under the Baker Act and Marchman Act because it provides a legal framework for individuals who are struggling

Family and Professional Guardianship

with mental health or substance abuse disorders.

The criteria for involuntary examination serve as a guide for healthcare professionals and law enforcement officials to identify individuals who need assistance and to ensure that they receive the appropriate care.

Furthermore, understanding the criteria for the involuntary examination can also help individuals and their loved ones understand their legal rights during the examination period. The Baker Act and Marchman Act both provide specific guidelines for how individuals should be treated during the examination process, as well as their rights to contest the examination if they so choose.

Another point I wanted to make in this chapter is that while guardianship plays a crucial role in protecting individuals with mental health disorders, substance abuse disorders, and elderly or vulnerable adults, it may not always be the best option.

Alternatives such as Durable Power of Attorney and Designation of Health Care Surrogate may be more appropriate in certain situations. It is important to explore all options and seek legal

6. Determining When Guardianship is Needed

advice to ensure that the individual's rights and interests are protected.

By understanding the criteria for involuntary examination, the role of family guardians, and the alternatives to guardianship, individuals and families can make informed decisions that provide the necessary care and support while protecting the individual's rights and interests.

7. Placement of Incapacitated Persons and Costs

7.1. Overview

One of the most important decisions a guardian may have to make is where to place the incapacitated person. The placement decision can have significant consequences for the quality of life, health, and well-being of the incapacitated person.

I will begin with a case study concerning a hospital discharge demand and a family's distress. They had no available placement option and no money to pay for placement. But their beloved grandmother had a discharge order signed by a doctor at the hospital.

This chapter will explore placement options for incapacitated persons and the associated costs.

We will examine the opportunities, cost and potential risks associated with each option, such as the potential lack of support and supervision, possible exploitation risk and the difficulty in ensuring the incapacitated person receives the care they need.

The first placement option that we will explore is home or community placement. This option involves allowing the incapacitated person to remain in their own home or within their familiar community. This placement has the primary benefit of maintaining the person in familiar surroundings and allows them to maintain relationships with family and friends.

Independent living facilities can be used for persons that can generally handle their functions of daily living with minimal assistance but require some limited services. This solution involves allowing the person to live on their own or with other individuals who require minimal assistance.

Assisted living facilities (ALFs) are a popular placement option for incapacitated persons. These facilities provide a range of services and support for individuals who require assistance with daily activities, but who do not require the constant medical attention provided by a nursing home or skilled nursing facility.

7. Placement of Incapacitated Persons and Costs

Nursing homes are yet another placement option that is discussed in this chapter. Nursing homes provide 24-hour medical supervision and support for individuals who require a high level of care. This option comes with decreased independence and autonomy.

Skilled nursing facilities provide specialized medical care and support for individuals with complex medical needs, such as individuals with severe chronic conditions or those recovering from surgery. One benefit of skilled nursing facilities includes the potential for increased medical care and support.

I will also discuss placement services, which can be a helpful resource for families and guardians who are looking to place a family member or friend. These services provide information about placement options and can help guide guardians through the placement process. There is usually no cost for these services because they are paid by the residential centers.

Finally, I will discuss the costs of placement of incapacitated persons in Florida and provide examples of how costs vary depending on a range of factors, including the type of placement, level of care required, and location of the placement facility.

I believe that this chapter is a useful resource for guardians and families who are responsible for the care of an incapacitated person in Florida, as it provides guidance on the different types of placement options available and the factors to consider when making these decisions.

Case Study

An Unsafe Discharge: How to Manage a Hospital or Care Facility Discharge Request When There is No Place to Go.

My office often does free consultations to help families navigate the care and placement of loved ones.

An acquaintance made the referral. The hospital is preparing to discharge a patient with no place for her to go. The question for the family becomes, "what do we do now."

The caller was in distress, near tears. Her grandmother was in the hospital. They had received a call from the discharge planner with disturbing news. The discharge planner said the grandmother was being discharged from the hospital and they had to come pick her up.

This was not an unusual call, as hospital case managers are responsible for notification of

7. Placement of Incapacitated Persons and Costs

caregivers or family members to accept patients discharged from hospitals. What made this call disturbing was that there was no qualified caregiver available to care for the discharged patient. They had no place to go but continued to receive demanding calls from the hospital.

There are many reasons why a family member may be unable to provide care. These can include their own personal illness and financial situation, their own advanced age, a defiant patient, security, and elopement risk, the need for twenty-four-hour care requirements, work schedules, and more. These are just a few.

Prior to hospitalization the grandmother had lived alone in her private home. She had a fall in the home and was not able to get up. Luckily, her cell phone was nearby. She called a relative who came to help. She was transported by ambulance to the hospital. While in the hospital it was determined that she had cognitive disorders and recommended that she no longer live alone. She had dementia. Living alone was no longer an option. Moving her back home would make this an unsafe discharge. Her hospitalization and eventual discharge, as is often the case, had been sudden and unexpected.

Unsafe discharge from a hospital or other health care facilities is not allowed by Florida law, regardless of the reason presented by institutions. These laws are in place to prevent patient dumping.

I advised the family to notify the hospital that no safe discharge placement was available. This stopped the calls and allowed the family to plan for placement and funding for the placement.

The next steps involved locating an Assisted Living Facility (ALF) or Nursing facility and planning to fund the cost, estimated to be $3,200.00 monthly. Neither the grandmother nor family could afford this. Additionally, they did not have any idea about what an ALF was or how to find one that would accept her without payment.

The solution involved first notifying the hospital they could not make an unsafe discharge. This allowed the family to get advice on placement and funding the cost. Secondly, they would need to apply for Medicaid. This application to Medicaid would make the patient Medicaid pending, this is not an approval. However, there are ALF's and critical care facilities that will accept residents if they are Medicaid pending. Thirdly, they began a search for a placement. They requested that the hospital help. Hospitals often have mechanisms in place to conduct a search for placement facilities.

7. Placement of Incapacitated Persons and Costs

My office walked them through the lengthy application process for Medicaid; shortly after this they were pending. They still did not have a placement that would accept the Medicaid pending status. During their search, the hospital had agreed to search for placement. The hospital search produced a placement. It was determined that this was a safe discharge. The grandmother was discharged to the facility. It turned out that the facility was farther from the family than they would have liked.

The family began to follow up on the Medicaid application and once it is approved, they will search for placement closer to home.

7.2. Home or Community Placement

This is commonly called community-based placement. Home or community placement involves allowing incapacitated persons to remain in their own homes or within the community they are familiar with[12]. This option is often preferred by incapacitated people who wish to maintain their independence and remain in familiar surroundings. Home or community placement

---

[12] Weissert, W. G., et al. (1988). "The past and future of home-and community-based long-term care." The Milbank Quarterly: 309-388.

can be an ideal option for individuals who require minimal assistance with daily activities and can benefit from a supportive and caring environment.

This placement option can take many different forms, depending on the needs and circumstances of the incapacitated person. For example, some individuals may choose to live in their own homes with the support of a caregiver who visits regularly. Others may choose to live with family members or friends who can provide the necessary care and support. In some cases, individuals may choose to live in a community setting, such as a group home or assisted living facility, where they can receive the necessary care and support while still maintaining a degree of independence.

There are several benefits associated with home or community placement for incapacitated persons. Perhaps the most significant benefit is the ability of the incapacitated person to remain in familiar surroundings and maintain relationships with family and friends. This can be particularly important for individuals who may be experiencing feelings of isolation or loneliness. Home or community placement can also provide a greater sense of independence and autonomy, allowing the incapacitated person to continue to

7. Placement of Incapacitated Persons and Costs

make their own decisions and live life on their own terms.

However, this type of placement also comes with some potential drawbacks and risks that must be considered. For example, there may be a lack of support and supervision available in the home or community setting, which can be particularly problematic for individuals with complex medical needs or who require a high level of care. Additionally, there may be difficulty in ensuring that the incapacitated person receives the necessary care and support, particularly if they are living alone or with family members who are not able to provide the necessary level of care.

When considering home or community placement, there are several other factors that guardians and families should consider. First, they should consider the specific needs and circumstances of the incapacitated person, including their medical needs, level of independence, and social support system. They should also consider the availability of support and supervision in the home or community setting, as well as the potential for isolation and loneliness.

To ensure that home or community placement is successful, it is important to have a comprehensive plan in place that addresses the needs of the incapacitated person. This may include identifying a caregiver who can provide regular support and assistance, arranging for regular medical check-ups and monitoring, and ensuring that the incapacitated person has access to appropriate social support and activities.

In some cases, it may also be necessary to make modifications to the home or community environment in order to ensure that it is safe and supportive for the incapacitated person. This may include installing safety equipment such as grab bars or handrails, modifying the layout of the home to accommodate mobility needs, or providing additional support and supervision to ensure that the incapacitated person is able to navigate the home or community environment safely and independently.

When you use this option, it is of paramount importance that you coordinate care with the person's medical insurance provider. The health care provider can assist in creating a care plan, arranging for home health aide visits, transportation to and from medical appointments, free medical supplies, medication management, along with home visits from nurses and medical doctors. Of course, this all depended on the provider and type of coverage.

7.3. Independent Living

Independent living is a placement that can be a home placement but is most often at a facility that is established as an Independent Living Facility.

This option for incapacitated persons allows them to live in an apartment or home-like setting while receiving minimal assistance with the activities of daily living.

This placement option is particularly suitable for individuals who have a higher level of independence and require less support with daily living tasks[13]. In other words, independent living provides a supportive environment that enables incapacitated persons to maintain their independence and make their own decisions, while still receiving necessary support and assistance.

There are several benefits of independent living for incapacitated persons. First, it provides a greater sense of autonomy and control over their own lives. This can be particularly important for individuals who value their independence and

---

[13] Sousa, L. and D. Figueiredo (2002). "Dependence and independence among old persons–realities and myths." Reviews in Clinical Gerontology **12**(3): 269-273.

wish to continue to be involved in their own care. Independent living also allows incapacitated persons to remain in familiar surroundings, which can help to maintain relationships with family and friends and may reduce feelings of isolation and loneliness.

Second, independent living provides an opportunity for incapacitated persons to continue to engage in social activities and community events. This may help to improve their mental health and well-being and provide a sense of purpose and fulfillment.

Additionally, independent living can be a more cost-effective option than other types of placements, such as nursing homes or assisted living facilities.

However, independent living also comes with some potential drawbacks and risks that must be considered. One of the most significant risks associated with this option is the potential for increased social isolation and loneliness. This could be particularly problematic for individuals who live alone or who do not have access to regular social activities. Additionally, there may be difficulty if there are declines in health and safety concerns. This is of particular concern because there is often no one present around the clock.

7. Placement of Incapacitated Persons and Costs

As such, when considering independent living as a placement option, there are several factors that guardians and families should consider:

What are the specific needs and circumstances of the person, including their medical needs, level of independence, and social support system? They should also consider the availability of support and supervision in the independent environment, as well as the potential for isolation and loneliness.

To ensure that independent living is successful, it is important to have a comprehensive plan in place that addresses both current and anticipated future needs. This may include identifying a caregiver who can provide regular support and assistance, arranging for regular medical check-ups and monitoring, and ensuring that the incapacitated person has access to appropriate social support and activities.

One of the most important factors in ensuring the success of independent living is the availability of support and supervision. Incapacitated persons who live alone may require regular visits from a caregiver or home health aide in order to ensure that their medical needs are being met and they are receiving the necessary care and support. In some cases, it will be necessary to install safety equipment such as grab bars or handrails, or modify the layout of the home to accommodate mobility needs.

The benefits of placement in independent living facilities can include:

1. The ability to have a car if they can drive.
2. Medication dispensing
3. Meal preparation
4. House cleaning
5. Organized social activities
6. Community with persons of similar abilities
7. Larger residential accommodation, this not only allows for guest visits but also for a live-in care giver if needed.
8. Comfortable private home-like living arrangement

7.4. Assisted Living Facility (ALF)

Assisted Living Facilities (ALFs) are residential facilities that provide a supportive environment for incapacitated persons who require assistance with daily living activities[14] but do not require the level of medical care provided in a nursing home. Assisted living facilities offer a range of

---

[14] Ball, M. M., et al. (2004). "Independence in assisted living." Journal of Aging Studies **18**(4): 467-483.

7. Placement of Incapacitated Persons and Costs

services and amenities that enable incapacitated persons to maintain their independence and autonomy, while still receiving necessary support and assistance.

This placement option offers several benefits. Firstly, ALFs provide a safe and supportive environment that enables incapacitated persons to receive the necessary care and assistance without a significant level of independence.

Secondly, ALFs provide a range of services and amenities that can improve the quality of life for incapacitated persons. These may include regular social activities, transportation services, and access to medical care and assistance. More so, many ALFs offer a range of on-site amenities such as gyms, pools, and libraries, which can provide a sense of community for incapacitated persons.

Of course, like other options discussed, ALFs also come with some potential drawbacks. One of the most significant risks associated with this placement option is the potential for abuse and neglect, with incapacitated persons residing in ALFs being vulnerable to abuse or neglect by staff members or other residents. Additionally, there may be difficulties in ensuring that the incapacitated person receives the necessary care and support, particularly if the facility is understaffed or lacks appropriate supervision. Even in view of this the majority of clients are placed in assisted living facilities.

When considering ALFs as a placement option, families need to consider the circumstances of the incapacitated person, including their medical needs, level of independence, and social support system. They should also consider the availability of support and supervision within the facility, as well as the potential for abuse or neglect.

One of the most important factors in ensuring the success of assisted living facilities is the availability of support and supervision within the facility. This includes ensuring that there are appropriate staffing levels and that staff members are properly trained to provide care and assistance to incapacitated people.

7.5. Nursing Home

Nursing homes are residential facilities that provide a higher level of medical care and support than Assisted Living Facilities. Nursing homes are for incapacitated persons who require constant medical attention and assistance with daily living activities[15]. Nursing homes offer 24-hour medical supervision and support, and a range of services and amenities that can improve the quality of life for incapacitated persons.

This placement option provides a safe and supportive environment that enables incapacitated persons to receive the necessary medical care and assistance. This can be particularly important for individuals who have complex medical needs or who require constant supervision and support.

Secondly, nursing homes offer a range of services and amenities that can improve the quality of life for incapacitated persons. These may include regular social activities, transportation services, access to specialized medical care and assistance, and on-site amenities such as gyms, pools, and libraries.

One of the most significant risks associated with nursing homes is the potential for social isolation and loneliness. Incapacitated persons who reside in nursing homes may be separated from their families and communities, which can lead to feelings of isolation and loneliness. In addition,

---

[15] Alvarez, J. A. (2019). "Florida Needs to Protect Grandma & Grandpa.". Thomas L. Rev. **32**: 31.

there may be difficulties in ensuring that the incapacitated person receives the necessary care and support, particularly if the facility is understaffed or lacks appropriate supervision.

When considering nursing homes as a placement, families, in consultation with experts if needed, have to carefully assess medical needs, level of independence, and social support system. They should also consider the availability of support and supervision within the facility, as well as the potential for social isolation and loneliness.

One of the most important factors in ensuring the success of nursing homes is the availability of support and supervision within the facility. This includes ensuring that there are appropriate staffing levels and that staff members are properly trained to provide care and assistance to incapacitated persons.

7.6. Skilled Nursing Facility

A Skilled Nursing Facility (SNF) is a residential facility that provides the highest level of medical care and support. This is for persons who require constant medical attention and assistance with daily living activities. Skilled nursing facilities offer 24-hour medical supervision and support,

7. Placement of Incapacitated Persons and Costs

and a range of specialized services and amenities that can improve the quality of life for incapacitated persons, which may include access to specialized medical equipment and treatments, specialized rehabilitation services, and specialized care for individuals with specific medical conditions or needs[16].

Like in the case of standard nursing homes, the decision to place someone in an SNF must be based on careful consideration of the specific needs and circumstances of the incapacitated person, including their medical needs, level of independence, and social support system.

Deciding on whether a decapacitated person may need to be placed in a nursing home or an SNF requires understanding the differences between the two. Nursing homes are long-term care facilities. Some consider them as less restrictive than hospitals. They provide a range of services semilunar to hospitals but for people who do not require the level of medical care provided in a hospital.

---

[16] Gonzalez, L. (2022). "Long-term care options in Florida: Their availability by county demographics." <u>Journal of Racial and Ethnic Health Disparities</u> **9**(2): 698-707.

They help with activities such as bathing, dressing, and toileting, as well as access to medical care and rehabilitation services. Nursing homes also offer social and recreational activities to promote social interaction and help maintain cognitive function.

Based on the considerations above, it follows that nursing homes are generally better suited for incapacitated persons who require long-term care and support for chronic medical conditions or disabilities.

7.7. Using Professional Placement Services

When seeking a suitable placement for an incapacitated person, guardians and families can benefit from utilizing Professional Placement Services.

Professional Placement Services are companies that locate and assist with placement. The primary benefit of these companies is they generally know of most of the facilities in an area. They can match placement with the level of care required. Additionally, their fees are covered by the facility if you use a facility they have located for you.

These services can provide invaluable support and guidance in identifying suitable placement

7. Placement of Incapacitated Persons and Costs

options based on the specific needs and circumstances of the incapacitated person. A placement service can also assist with contracts, navigating the complex legal and financial requirements and can often negotiate the best monthly and registration fees.

Placement services typically provide a range of services, including conducting assessments of the incapacitated person's needs, identifying suitable placement options based on those needs, providing guidance and support in making placement decisions, and assisting with the application and admission process for chosen placement options. These services may also provide ongoing support and advocacy throughout the placement process to ensure that the incapacitated person receives the necessary care and support.

The key benefit of using a placement service is the ability to access a wide range of options that may not be readily available to the general public. More specifically, placement services typically have extensive networks and partnerships with a variety of placement options, including nursing homes, assisted living facilities, and skilled nursing facilities. This can provide guardians and families with access to specialized placement options that meet the unique needs and circumstances of the incapacitated person.

Here are some of the key components of the assessment process for placement services:

1. **In-Person Visit:** The assessment process typically begins with an in-person visit with the individual. During this visit, the placement service provider may gather information about the individual's daily living activities, the physical layout of the living space, and any equipment or devices that are currently being used to support the individual's needs.

2. **Medical Records and Care Plans:** The placement service provider may also review the individual's medical records and care plans to gather information about their medical conditions, medications, and other treatments. This information can help to identify any specialized medical needs or requirements that may need to be addressed in the placement process.

3. **Discussions with Family Members and Medical Professionals:** Conducting discussions with family members and medical professionals who are involved in the individual's care can provide additional insight into the individual's needs and preferences, as well as any challenges or

concerns that may need to be addressed in the placement process.

4. **Functional Assessment:** The placement service provider may conduct a functional assessment to evaluate the individual's ability to perform daily living activities, such as bathing, dressing, and toileting. This can help to identify any areas where the individual may require additional support or assistance in their daily routine.

5. **Cognitive Assessment:** For individuals with cognitive impairments, the placement service provider may conduct a cognitive assessment to evaluate the individual's cognitive function, including memory, language, and problem-solving skills.

6. **Social Assessment:** The placement service provider may evaluate the individual's social needs and preferences. This can help to identify any opportunities for social interaction and engagement that may be important for the individual's well-being. The assessment process can also help to ensure that the placement process is tailored to the individual's specific requirements and that any

specialized medical or daily living needs are addressed in the placement process.

When considering using placement services, you will want to carefully research and select a reputable and reliable provider. Guardians and families should consider factors such as the provider's experience and expertise, their range of services, their network of placement options, and their reputation within the industry.

If you have decided to seek a suitable placement option for an incapacitated person, there are several types of placement services available that can provide support and guidance in the placement process. These placement services vary in their scope of services and the types of placement options they offer. Here are some of the main types of placement services:

1. **Government Agencies:** Government agencies can provide placement services for incapacitated persons. These agencies may offer a range of services, including assessments, guidance on placement options, and assistance with the application and admission process for chosen placement options. Government agencies may also provide financial assistance for eligible incapacitated persons.

7. Placement of Incapacitated Persons and Costs

2. **Nonprofit Organizations:** Nonprofit organizations can provide placement services for individuals with specific medical conditions or disabilities. Some of these organizations offer specialized expertise in identifying placement options that meet the unique needs of individuals with specific medical conditions.

3. **Private Placement Agencies:** Private placement agencies are for-profit companies that specialize in identifying suitable placement options for incapacitated persons. These agencies typically have extensive networks and partnerships with a variety of placement options, including nursing homes, assisted living facilities, and skilled nursing facilities. Private placement agencies may provide a range of services, including assessments, guidance on placement options, and assistance with the application and admission process for chosen placement options.

4. **Referral Services:** Referral services are companies that provide information and referral services for individuals seeking placement options for incapacitated persons. These services typically provide information on a variety of placement options, including nursing homes, assisted

living facilities, and skilled nursing facilities, and may provide guidance on selecting the most suitable option based on the individual's needs.

- **Senior Housing Advisors:** Senior housing advisors are professionals who specialize in identifying suitable housing options for seniors and incapacitated persons. These advisors may provide services such as assessments, guidance on placement options, and assistance with the application and admission process for chosen placement options. Senior housing advisors may have specialized expertise in identifying placement options that meet the unique needs of seniors and incapacitated persons.

If you plan to use a placement service in Florida, here are some resources you might find helpful:

- **Florida Department of Elder Affairs**[17]: The Florida Department of Elder Affairs provides a variety of services for older adults — assistance in finding placement options for seniors and individuals with disabilities.

---

[17] https://elderaffairs.org/

7. Placement of Incapacitated Persons and Costs

- **Elder Options**[18]: Elder Options is a nonprofit organization that provides a variety of services for seniors and their families, including information and referral services for placement options.

- **Visiting Angels**[19]: Visiting Angels is a national home care agency that provides a variety of services for seniors and individuals with disabilities, including placement options.

- **Home Care Assistance**[20]: Home Care Assistance is a national home care agency that provides a variety of services for seniors and individuals with disabilities.

- **Assisted Living Locators**[21]: Assisted Living Locators is a national referral service that provides information and assistance in finding suitable placement options for seniors and individuals with disabilities.

7.8. Costs of Placement of Incapacitated Persons in Florida

---

[18] https://agingresources.org/
[19] https://www.visitingangels.com/
[20] https://homecareassistance.com/
[21] https://assistedlivinglocators.com/

The costs of placement options for incapacitated persons in Florida can vary depending on the type of placement, level of care required, and location of the placement facility. Florida has a large senior population, which can impact the availability and affordability of placement options for incapacitated persons. Here are some of the key factors that can impact the costs of placement for incapacitated persons in Florida:

1. **Type of Placement:** Nursing homes and skilled nursing facilities are more expensive than assisted living facilities or home care services.

2. **Level of Care:** Individuals who require specialized medical care, such as those with chronic medical conditions or severe disabilities, may require more expensive care options that can increase the overall cost of care.

3 **Location:** Placement facilities in urban areas may be more expensive than those in rural areas, due to higher real estate and labor costs.

4. **Duration of Care:** Long-term care options, such as nursing homes or skilled nursing facilities, can be significantly 2014

Identifying affordable and sustainable placement options can be challenging. In many cases, navigating through the many placement options available will require communicating with several channels, including placement service providers, financial advisors, and insurance providers.

7.9. Chapter Summary

This chapter provides an overview of the different types of placement options available, including home or community placement, independent living, ALFs, nursing homes, SNFs, and placement services.

Clearly, there are benefits and drawbacks to each placement option. We can see that a recurrent consideration that needs to be taken when making a decision is the potential for an **increase or decrease in independence and autonomy**, the potential for an **increase or decrease in socialization and support**, and the **costs** associated with each option.

Another important takeaway from this chapter is that the costs of placement options for incapacitated persons can vary widely depending on a range of factors, including the type of placement, level of care required, and location of the placement facility. While I have provided some examples of costs in Florida, these examples are just that and are based on averages. The costs vary significantly depending on the discussed factors.

The goal of this chapter is to be a useful resource for guardians and families responsible for the care and placement of an incapacitated person in Florida, as it provides detailed information on the different placement options available, outlines the specific benefits and drawbacks of each option, and emphasizes the importance of considering factors such as costs and insurance coverage. This information should help readers to make more informed and effective decisions when it comes to the placement of incapacitated persons in Florida.

8. Funding for Care and Placement

8.1. Overview

An important aspect of guardianship is the funding for the care and placement of the incapacitated person. There are several different sources of funding that may be available for care and placement in guardianship cases in Florida.

This chapter will provide more detailed information on each of these sources of funding, as well as strategies for overcoming the challenges of securing funding. By understanding the different funding options and how to navigate the system, guardians can ensure that their loved ones receive the best possible care and placement while also protecting their financial interests. Here we will discuss several available funding sources briefly followed by a more in-depth review.

Retirement benefits are one such potential source. Seniors who have retired from work may be eligible for Social Security retirement benefits or pension benefits from their former employer. These benefits can be used to pay for the costs of care and placement.

Government programs are another potential source of funding. The two most commonly used programs in Florida are:

Medicare, which is federally funded, may provide most medically necessary services and supplies in hospitals, doctors' offices, and other health care facilities, including hospitalizations, physician visits, prescription drugs, preventive services, skilled nursing facility and home health care, and hospice care.

Medicaid, which is a state funded service, can be used to pay for a wide range of services, including long-term care in a nursing home or other facility, and may pay the balance of premiums not covered by Medicare. To be eligible for Medicaid, an individual must meet certain income and asset requirements.

Medicare can be used to pay for some of the costs of long-term care, such as skilled nursing care, but it does not cover all the costs. In some

8. Funding for Care and Placement

cases, individuals may need to supplement their Medicare coverage with other forms of funding, such as Medicaid or private programs.

Private programs are another potential source of funding for care and placement in guardianship cases.

Insurance policies, for instance, such as long-term care insurance or life insurance policies with long-term care riders, are one such option. Common insurance policy riders that can assist with the cost of care include End-of-life riders which are additional benefits that can be added to a life insurance policy. These riders provide additional coverage for the policyholder and their family in the event of a terminal illness or death. Several of the most common end-of-life riders are:

Accelerated death benefit rider: This rider allows the policyholder to receive a portion of the death benefit while they are still alive if they are diagnosed with a terminal illness.

Waiver of premium rider: This rider waives the policyholder's premium payments if they become disabled or seriously ill.

Long-term care rider: This rider provides coverage for long-term care expenses if the policyholder becomes unable to care for themselves.

Child rider: This rider provides coverage for the policyholder's children.

Annuities are financial products that provide a regular stream of income and can also be used to pay for care and placement. Individual retirement accounts (IRAs) are retirement accounts that provide tax advantages and can also be used to fund care and placement.

Mutual funds are investment vehicles that pool money from multiple investors to purchase securities and are another option to consider. Bank accounts and other assets can be used to fund care and placement through the use of trusts or other arrangements.

While there are several different sources of funding that may be available for care and placement in guardianship cases, there are also several challenges that may arise when trying to secure funding. These challenges include eligibility requirements, the complexity of navigating different programs, and the need to balance the interests of the incapacitated person with the interests of the guardian.

Eligibility requirements can be a significant challenge when trying to secure funding for care and placement. Many government programs,

8. Funding for Care and Placement

such as Medicaid, have strict income and asset requirements that must be met before an individual can qualify for benefits. This can be particularly challenging for individuals who have significant assets or income that exceed the eligibility thresholds. Medicaid is discussed in detail in the next section.

The complexity of navigating different programs is another challenge that can arise when trying to secure funding for care and placement. Each program has its own set of rules, regulations, and application procedures, which can be difficult to navigate, especially for individuals who are already dealing with the stress and complexity of a guardianship case.

Finally, there is often tension between the interests of the incapacitated person and the interests of the guardian when it comes to funding for care and placement. Guardians are typically appointed to act in the best interests of the incapacitated person, but they may also have their own financial interests to consider. For example, some guardians may choose a care facility that is less expensive, even if it may not be the choice of the family for the incapacitated person.

8.2. Retirement Benefits

Retirement benefits are one of the potential sources of funding for care and placement in guardianship cases. Seniors who have retired from work may be eligible for Social Security retirement benefits or pension benefits from their former employer. These benefits can be used to pay for the costs of care and placement.

Social Security retirement benefits are a federal program that provides financial support to individuals who have retired from work. The amount of benefit received depends on a variety of factors, including the individual's earnings history and the age at which they begin receiving benefits. The earliest age at which an individual can receive Social Security retirement benefits is 62. But the longer they wait, the higher their monthly benefit will be. On the other hand, if they take it early and live longer, they can make up for this over time. I took it at age 62, now, at 72, I am still going strong.

Social Security retirement benefits can be used to fund care and placement in several ways. First, the benefits can be used to pay for the costs of in-home care, such as a home health aide or a personal care assistant. Second, the benefits can be used to pay for the costs of care in a nursing home or other long-term care facility. Finally, the benefits can be used to supplement other sources of funding, such as Medicaid or private insurance. With careful planning, a person may have both Medicare and Medicaid.

This is called dual Medicare/Medicaid. Many people miss this added benefit due to a lack of professional advice on how to apply and how to protect their income and assets from the asset and income limits. Later I will show you how this is done. But for now, let's say once and for all, yes, there are legal ways to qualify for Medicaid and keep large incomes and assets.

Pension benefits are retirement benefits provided by an individual's former employer. The amount of money one might receive and the specific benefits received depends on a variety of factors, including the individual's earnings history, the length of time they worked for the employer, and the terms of the pension plan.

Pension benefits can be used to fund care and placement in several ways. First, the benefits can be used to pay for the costs of in-home care, such as a home health aide or a personal care assistant. Second, the benefits can be used to pay for the costs of care in a nursing home or other long-term care facility. Finally, the benefits can be used to supplement other sources of funding, such as Medicaid or private insurance.

When using pension benefits with Medicare, you will have to consider the income limits for Medicare. If the pension income places you over the Medicare or Medicaid income limit, then it will have to be protected from the income limit in order for you to qualify.

Effective Jan 1, 2022, the applicant's gross monthly income may not exceed $2,523.00. The applicant may retain $130 per month for personal expenses. However, even having excess income is not necessarily a deal-breaker in terms of Medicaid eligibility.

401(k) plans and individual retirement accounts (IRAs) are retirement savings accounts that allow individuals to save money for retirement on a tax-deferred basis. These accounts can be used to fund care and placement in guardianship cases.

If an individual has a 401(k) plan or an IRA, they can withdraw money from the account to pay for the costs of care and placement. However, withdrawals from these accounts are subject to income tax and may also be subject to an early withdrawal penalty if the individual is under the age of 59 ½.

8. Funding for Care and Placement

Reverse mortgages are another potential source of funding for care and placement in guardianship cases. A reverse mortgage is a loan that allows homeowners aged 62 or older to convert a portion of their home equity into cash. The loan is repaid when the homeowner sells the home or passes away.

Reverse mortgages can be used to fund care and placement in several ways. First, the cash obtained from the reverse mortgage can be used to pay for the costs of in-home care or the costs of care in a long-term care facility. Second, the reverse mortgage can be used to supplement other sources of funding, such as Medicaid or private insurance.

While retirement benefits can be a potential source of funding for care and placement in guardianship cases, there are also several challenges that can arise. One of the biggest challenges is the limited amount of funds available. Social Security retirement benefits and pension benefits are typically not enough to cover the full costs of care and placement, and other sources of funding may need to be used to supplement these benefits.

Another challenge is the complexity of navigating the various retirement benefit programs. Each program has its own rules and eligibility requirements, and it can be difficult to determine which benefits an individual is eligible for and how to apply for them. Additionally, some retirement benefits, such as Social Security retirement benefits, may be subject to income tax, which can further reduce the amount of funds available.

Despite these challenges, there are several strategies that guardians can use to overcome them and successfully use retirement benefits to fund care and placement. One strategy is to explore all available retirement benefit options and determine which benefits an individual is eligible for. This may involve consulting with a financial planner or an elder law attorney to fully understand the options available.

Finally, it is important for guardians to prioritize the well-being of the incapacitated person over their own financial interests when using retirement benefits to fund care and placement. This may involve choosing a care facility or in-home care provider that provides the best possible care, even if it is more expensive.

By understanding the challenges and strategies for overcoming them, guardians can successfully use retirement benefits to fund the best possible care and placement for their loved ones. It is often best that guardians consult with professionals such as financial planners and elder law attorneys to fully understand the various options available and to make informed decisions that prioritize the well-being of the incapacitated person.

8.3. Medicaid

Medicaid is a joint federal and state program that provides health care coverage to eligible individuals with low income or disabilities.[22] Medicaid can be a valuable source of funding for care and placement in guardianship cases.

Medicaid is a means-tested program, which means that eligibility is based on income and assets. The program is jointly funded by the federal government and the states, and each state administers its own Medicaid program, subject to federal regulations. In Florida, Medicaid is administered by the Florida Agency for Health Care Administration. Application for Medicaid can be filed in person or online at https://www.myflorida.com/accessflorida . I want to mention this one point now. If you qualify for Social Security

---

[22] Shadowen, H. and A. J. Barnes (2022). "Medicaid can and should play an active role in advancing health equity."

Supplemental Income (SSI), you qualify for Medicaid.

Medicaid covers a wide range of medical services, including doctor visits, hospital care, prescription drugs, and long-term care. In some cases, Medicaid can also cover the costs of in-home care.

To be eligible for Medicaid in Florida, individuals must meet certain income and asset requirements. The income and asset thresholds vary depending on the individual's age, disability status, and other factors. For example, a single individual applying for Nursing Home Medicaid in 2023 in Florida must have "an income under $2,742 per month and assets under $2,000, and must require the level of care provided in a nursing home facility[23]."

Individuals who are over the income and asset thresholds may still be eligible for Medicaid through a process called "spend down." Spend down allows individuals to subtract their medical expenses from their income to bring their income below the Medicaid threshold. This process

---

[23] Aging, A. C. o. (2023). "Florida Medicaid Eligibility: 2023 Income & Assets Limits." Retrieved 04/03, 2023, from https://www.medicaidplanningassistance.org/medicaid-eligibility-florida/.

8. Funding for Care and Placement

can be complicated, and it may be helpful to consult with an attorney or other professional to navigate the process.

While the basic application of spend down is to demonstrate net income at or below the Medicaid income limit. Be aware that in many cases spend down is not enough to get the income down to the Medicaid income limit. You may make this a first option but know that there are other strategies as well.

Among these added strategies, remember that giving money and assets away is not one of them. There is a five-year look-back by Medicaid to see if income or assets have been given away or disposed. This includes a sale for less than fair market value. However, there remain many other approved plans. Never a week goes by that I do not look on in horror as I see so many in need who are missing this crucial benefit simply because of the lack of knowledge about how the application works.

In fact, there are so many ways to meet the income and asset limit that I am amazed that this limit still exists. Indeed, there is a move afoot to eliminate both. California is leading the way in this effort. California has eliminated both the income limit and the asset limit for Medicaid qualifications. The limits serve one purpose - that is to impoverish applicants.

Among the approved strategies, we use the following. You can find the complete list and more detailed descriptions at this website: Planning Techniques to Help Gain Medicaid Eligibility (medicaidplanningassistance.org).

- *Medicaid Compliant Pool Trust* – This is a trust that is irrevocable but can be changed so that it can be used for services not covered by Medicaid. They are used to shield income for the Medicaid income limit. Two companies providing Pool Trust in Florida include Aged Inc. and Guardian Trust.

- *ABLE Account* - An ABLE account is a tax-advantaged savings account for individuals with disabilities and their families, authorized by the ABLE Act of 2014. ABLE accounts protect resources from affecting eligibility for Medicaid or SSI, as long as they are used for qualified disability-related purposes.

- *Special Needs Trust (SNT)* - A special needs trust (SNT) is a legal arrangement that allows a trustee to manage and distribute funds for the benefit of a person with a disability. SNTs protect resources from affecting eligibility for Medicaid or SSI, as long as they are used for qualified disability-related purposes

- *Irrevocable Funeral Trust* – This trust is a legal arrangement that allows you to set aside money for your funeral and burial expenses in advance. The money is held in a trust fund that is owned by an insurance company or a funeral service provider. The trust fund pays for your funeral and burial costs when you die, according to your wishes. The primary benefit of the trust is that money held in the trust is not counted toward your asset limit for Medicaid eligibility purposes.

- **Monthly Maintenance Needs Allowance** (MMNA). When only one spouse of a married couple applies for Nursing Home Medicaid or a Home and Community Based Services (HCBS) Medicaid Waiver, certain Spousal Protections apply to ensure the community spouse does not become impoverished.

The community spouse, also called a well spouse, is the non-applicant spouse. In

2023, the community spouse is generally permitted up to $148,620 in countable assets, while the Medicaid applicant is usually only allowed $2,000. Additionally, if a spouse is in a nursing home and you apply for Medicaid for them, you may be entitled to keep a portion of their Social Security income as part of your Monthly Maintenance Needs Allowance.

This is the amount of income that Medicaid allows a spouse to keep for living expenses without affecting the incapacitated spouse eligibility for Medicaid.

The MMNA varies by state, but in 2023, the minimum MMNA in Florida was $2,155 and the maximum MMNA was $3,435. If the well spouse income is less than the minimum MMNA set by the state, they may keep some of the incapacitated spouse's income to bring them up to that level. The rest of their income, minus a small Personal Needs Allowance (PNA), must be paid to the nursing home as their share of cost.

For example, if you live in Florida, where the MMNA is $2,155 and the PNA is $130, and the well spouse income is $1,500 and

8. Funding for Care and Placement

your incapacitated spouse income is $1,000, the well spouse may keep $655 of your other spouse income to bring your total income to $2,155. The incapacitated spouse will keep $130 as her PNA, and the remaining $215 will be paid to the nursing home.

- *Medicaid Compliant Annuities* - Annuities must be irrevocable (impossible to alter or terminate), must be immediate (payments start right away), and the monthly payments must not exceed the life expectancy of the recipient. Spousal annuities are not an option in all states.

- *Spend Down Excess Assets* - Options include making home modifications and improvements, such as adding a chair lift or putting on a new roof, purchasing medical devices that are not covered by insurance, like dentures, and paying off one's mortgage or credit card debt. One may not gift assets or sell them for less than fair-market value.

- *Medicaid Divorces* - Medicaid Divorce is the legal termination of a marriage of a couple in which only one spouse applies for long-term care Medicaid.

- *Spousal Refusal* - Non-applicant spouses, while legally obligated to help cover the cost of Medicaid long-term care for their applicant spouses, can still refuse to make their assets available for this purpose.

- *Medicaid Asset Protected Trust* - A Medicaid Asset Protection Trust (MAPT) is a type of irrevocable (irreversible) trust that protects assets from being counted towards Medicaid's asset limit.

- *Lady Bird Deeds* - Lady Bird Deeds allow Medicaid applicants to protect their home for their adult children or other loved ones as inheritance. With this type of life estate deed, the Medicaid recipient still has ownership over their home as long as they are living.

- *Child Caregiver Exception* - The Child Caregiver Exception allows Medicaid applicants to transfer their home to their healthy adult child. The child must have lived with their aging parent for a minimum of 2 years immediately prior to the parent's nursing home admittance.

- *Sibling Exception* - The Sibling Exception permits Medicaid applicants to transfer their home to a sibling who also has equity interest in their home.

- *Spousal Income Transfer* - The Sibling Exception permits Medicaid applicants to transfer their home to a sibling who also has equity interest in their home.

- *Qualified Income Trust / Miller Trust* - Income over the limit is allocated into a qualified irrevocable (unchangeable and unconcealable) income or Miller Trust, no longer counting towards Medicaid's income limit.

- *Income Spend Down* - Persons become eligible for Medicaid once they have spent their income down to the Medically Needy Income Limit.

Many people will have plans that include one or more of these planning options depending on their needs. This process can be complicated and if you are not familiar with them it is recommended that you get advice from a professional with experience in Medicaid planning.

Medicaid may be the single most important tool for planning for care and placement. Don't overlook it because of lack of familiarity, misinformation or by thinking it is only for the poor or indigent. Properly done it can pay up to half the cost of long-term care placement in Nursing Homes, Assisted Living Facilities and Skilled Nursing Homes. It can be used to fund care and placement in several ways.

Medicaid can be used to pay for the costs of long-term care. Medicaid will cover the full cost of care for eligible individuals, except for a small monthly co-payment.

Medicaid can be used to pay for the costs of in-home care. In-home care services can include personal care assistance, home health aides, and other services that allow individuals to receive care in their own homes. Medicaid will cover the costs of these services for eligible individuals.

Medicaid can be used to supplement other sources of funding, such as retirement benefits or private insurance. For example, if an individual is receiving Social Security retirement benefits but the benefits do not cover the full cost of care, Medicaid can be used to supplement the benefits.

Even if you are approved, be aware that one of the challenges is the limited availability of long-term care facilities that accept Medicaid. Not all nursing homes and other long-term care facilities accept Medicaid, and those that do may have waiting lists or other restrictions.

One strategy is to research and identify long-term care facilities that accept Medicaid. This can involve contacting facilities directly, researching online, or working with a placement agency that specializes in Medicaid-eligible facilities. Additionally, you can seek the services of professional placement agencies.

8.4. Medicare

When most people think of Medicare, they think of it as retirement income for seniors. But it is much, much more. On the face, there are so many parts that it seems impossible to navigate.

While it is beyond the scope of this book to provide the full breath of Medicare under Social Security, I do plan to provide an overview of the program. For further information, I refer you to their website, https://ssa.gov or to professionals who work in this area.

Let's talk about the Medicare federal health insurance program and coverage, its's parts and what it covers. The program is divided into several parts.

Part A, which covers hospital care, skilled nursing care, and hospice care.

Part B, which covers doctor visits, medical equipment, and other medical services.

Part C, which allows individuals to receive coverage through a private insurance company.

Part D, which provides prescription drug coverage.

To be eligible for Medicare insurance, individuals must be aged 65 or older, or have certain disabilities. Individuals must also be either a U.S. citizen or permanent legal resident who has lived in the U.S. for at least five years.

Medicare coverage can be used to fund care and placement in several ways. First, Medicare Part A can be used to pay for the costs of hospital care, including care received in a long-term care facility. Medicare Part A can also be used to pay for hospice care.

Medicare Part B can also be used to pay for doctor visits and other medical services, including in-home care services such as home health aides and physical therapy, and medical equipment such as wheelchairs and oxygen.

8. Funding for Care and Placement

Medicare Part C, also known as Medicare Advantage, can be used to fund care and placement. Medicare Advantage plans are offered by private insurance companies and provide coverage that is similar to Parts A and B, as well as additional benefits such as vision, dental, and hearing care. Some Medicare Advantage plans may also offer coverage for in-home care services.

Finally, Medicare Part D can be used to pay for prescription drugs, which can be a significant expense for individuals who require long-term care.

Using Medicare is not without challenges. One of the biggest challenges is the limited scope of coverage it provides. For example, Medicare Part A covers only a limited amount of time in a long-term care facility, and Medicare Part B may only cover a portion of the cost of in-home care services.

Another challenge is the complexity of navigating the Medicare program. Each part and plan has its own rules and requirements, and it can be difficult to determine which parts and plans an individual is eligible for and how to apply for them. There are several strategies that guardians can use to successfully use Medicare to fund care and placement. One strategy is to explore all available Medicare options and determine which parts and plans an individual is eligible for. This may involve consulting with a Medicare specialist or other professional to fully understand the options available.

Another strategy is to supplement Medicare coverage with other sources of funding, such as Medicaid or private insurance. For example, if Medicare Part A only covers a limited amount of time in a nursing home, Medicaid can be used to supplement the coverage and pay for the remaining costs. This planning is called dual Medicare.

For detailed information on the full scope of Medicare, please visit their government website or seek experienced council from professionals who work in this space.

8.5. Railroad Retirement Benefits

We have found that this is an often overlooked and underused benefit. As I have looked for benefits for many of our clients, I have been amazed at how many have, at one time in their life, worked for the railroad. If you or someone you know worked for the railroad, then you should apply. With incapacitated persons with Alzheimer's, their short-term memory will be fuzzy

8. Funding for Care and Placement

or gone, but just try to talk to them about times long ago; you may be surprised. But that is how we often learn that they worked for the railroad.

Railroad Retirement Benefits are available to railroad employees and their dependents and can be a source of funding for care and placement. Semilunar to Social Security, the program covers retirement, survivor, and disability benefits to eligible railroad employees and their dependents.[24] More specifically, Railroad Retirement Benefits are a form of social insurance provided by the U.S. Railroad Retirement Board.

The Railroad Retirement Program is funded by a payroll tax paid by railroad employers and employees and is separate from the Social Security program.

To be eligible for Railroad Retirement Benefits, individuals must have worked for a railroad employer for a certain number of years and have paid into the Railroad Retirement system through payroll taxes. The number of years required for eligibility depends on the individual's age and occupation, but generally ranges from 10 to 30 years.

---

[24] Pesner, M. (2021). "Public Pensions and Retirement: Evidence from the Railroad Retirement Act." Manuscript, Vanderbilt University.

Railroad Retirement Benefits can be used to fund care and placement in several ways. First, they can be used to pay for the costs of long-term care. The amount of benefit money available will depend on the individual's length of service and the amount of payroll taxes they have paid into the Railroad Retirement system.

Second, Railroad Retirement Benefits can be used to pay for in-home care services, such as home health aides and physical therapy. The availability of benefits for these services will depend on the individual's specific situation and the type of care required.

Railroad Retirement Benefits can also be used to supplement other sources of funding, such as Medicaid or private insurance. For example, if an individual is receiving supplemental Medicaid from the state but the benefits still do not cover the full cost of care, Railroad Retirement Benefits can be used to supplement those additional costs.

One of the biggest challenges to using Railroad Retirement is the limited availability of benefits for certain types of care. For example, these benefits may not cover all of the costs of in-home care services.

8.6. Social Security Benefits

Similar to Medicare, the full scope of Social Security benefits and services are beyond the scope of this book and you are encouraged to seek counsel from experienced professionals in this space. Please visit their government website at http://www.ssa.gov .

Social Security benefits are broken down into four categories. They are retirement, survivor, disability, and supplemental social security (SSI) benefits. Each can play vital roles in a well-crafted care plan for persons with disabilities and who are incapacitated or at risk of incapacitation.

Social Security is a federal program that provides benefits to retired and disabled workers, as well as to their dependents and survivors. There are several types of Social Security benefits that may be available to fund care and placement, including retirement benefits, survivor benefits, and disability benefits. Each type of benefit has its own eligibility requirements and rules, which we will discuss in detail below.

8.6.1. Retirement Benefits

Social Security is a federal program that provides financial support to eligible individuals who have reached retirement age.

Family and Professional Guardianship

To be eligible for Social Security retirement benefits, individuals must have earned a certain number of "credits" by paying into the Social Security system through payroll taxes. Forty (40) credits are required for eligibility.

Once an individual becomes eligible for Social Security retirement benefits, they can choose to begin receiving benefits as early as age 62 or as late as age 70. The amount of benefit dollars received depends on several factors, including the individual's earnings history, the age at which they begin receiving benefits, and whether they continue to work while receiving benefits.

Social Security retirement benefits can be used to fund care and placement in several ways. First, retirement benefits can be used to pay for the costs of long-term care. The dollar amount and benefits available will depend on the individual's earnings history and the age at which they begin receiving benefits.

Second, retirement benefits can be used to pay for in-home care services, such as home health aides and physical therapy. The availability of benefits for these services will depend on the individual's specific situation and the type of care required.

Third, retirement benefits can be used to supplement other sources of funding, such as Medicaid or private insurance.

8.6.2. Survivor Benefits

Social Security Survivor benefits are a federal program that provides financial support to eligible individuals who have experienced the loss of a spouse or parent. The dollar amount and benefits received depends on factors such as the deceased individual's earnings history and the age and relationship of the survivor.

To be eligible for survivor benefits, individuals must have a qualifying relationship with the deceased individual, such as being a spouse, child, or dependent parent.

Social Security survivor benefits can be used to fund care and placement in several ways. First, survivor benefits can be used to pay for the costs of long-term care.

Survivor benefits can also be used to pay for in-home care services, such as home health aides and physical therapy. The availability of benefits for these services will depend on the individual's specific situation and the type of care required.

Third, survivor benefits can be used to supplement other sources of funding, such as Medicaid or private insurance. Social Security survivor benefits may not cover all of the costs of in-home care services.

8.6.3. Disability Benefits (SSDI)

Social Security Disability Insurance (SSDI) benefits are a federal program that provides financial support to eligible individuals who have a disability that prevents them from working. More specifically, these benefits are available to those who have a disability that prevents them from working for at least 12 months or that is expected to result in death. To be eligible for disability benefits, individuals must have earned a certain number of "credits" by paying into the Social Security system through payroll taxes.

Once an individual becomes eligible for Social Security Disability benefits, they can begin receiving benefits after a five-month waiting period. The dollar amount and benefits received depends on several factors, including the individual's earnings history and the severity of their disability.

Social Security disability benefits can be used to fund care and placement in multiple ways. First, disability benefits can be used to pay for the costs of long-term care. The benefits available will depend on the individual's earnings history and the severity of their disability.

Disability benefits can also be used to pay for in-home care services, such as home health aides and physical therapy. The availability of benefits for these services will depend on the individual's specific situation and the type of care required. Third, disability benefits can be used to supplement other sources of funding, such as Medicaid or private insurance. Social Security disability benefits may not cover all of the costs of in-home care services.

8.6.4. The Supplemental Security Income (SSI)

Supplemental Security Income (SSI) is a federal program that provides financial assistance to individuals who have low income and limited resources and who are blind, aged, or disabled. SSI provides a monthly cash benefit to help eligible individuals meet basic needs such as food, clothing, and shelter. Eligibility for SSI is based on factors that include income, resources, and disability status.

SSI can be used to fund care and placement in several ways. SSI benefits can be used to pay for the costs of long-term care. The amount of benefits available will depend on the individual's income and resources, as well as the cost of care.

SSI benefits can be used to supplement other sources of funding, such as Medicaid or private insurance. For example, if an individual is receiving Medicaid benefits but the benefits do not cover the full cost of care, SSI benefits can be used to supplement the benefits. Additionally, in Florida, if you qualify for SSI, you automatically qualify for Medicaid.

8.6.5. Other programs

Aside from Social Security retirement benefits, Survivor benefits, Disability benefits, and Supplemental Security Income (SSI), there are several other programs that can provide funding for care and placement in guardianship cases.

Veterans' benefits, for example, are available to eligible veterans and their dependents. These benefits can include health care, disability compensation, and pension benefits. In terms of funding for care and placement, the Aid and Attendance pension benefit may be particularly relevant.
This benefit provides financial assistance to veterans and their surviving spouses who require

the aid and attendance of another person to complete daily activities. This benefit can be used to pay for long-term care.

Workers' compensation is a state-run insurance program that provides benefits to employees who are injured or become ill as a result of their job. These benefits can include medical care, wage replacement, and vocational rehabilitation. Workers' compensation benefits can be used to fund care and placement in cases where the incapacitated person's condition is a result of a work-related injury or illness.

In some cases, individuals may receive a settlement or award as a result of a personal injury lawsuit. These settlements or awards can be used to fund care and placement in cases where the incapacitated person's condition is a result of the injury or illness that was the subject of the lawsuit.

Private insurance, such as long-term care insurance or disability insurance, can also be a potential source of funding for care and placement in guardianship cases. Long-term care insurance policies can provide benefits for nursing home care, assisted living facilities, and in-home care services. Disability insurance policies can provide benefits to individuals who are unable to work due to a disability, which can be used to fund care and placement.

Trusts can also be used to fund care and placement in guardianship cases. For example, a properly structured Medicaid compliant Special Needs Trust can be established to provide financial support for an individual with a disability or incapacity while still allowing them to qualify for government benefits such as Medicaid or SSI. Assets held in these types of trust are not counted against the Medicaid asset limit. Assets held in the trust remain available to pay for the care and needs of the applicant that are not covered by benefits programs such as Medicaid or Medicare.

Accessing any of these programs does not come without challenges. For example, eligibility requirements for veterans' benefits and workers' compensation can be complex and difficult to navigate. Personal injury settlements may be unpredictable in terms of the amount and timing of the award.

Private insurance policies may have limitations on the types of care that are covered or may not provide enough coverage to fully fund care and placement. Trusts can also be complex to set up and manage and may not be an option for all individuals. Because of the complexities of these programs, it is always recommended that you seek out help from professionals in the various areas of interest.

8.7. Private Programs

In addition to government programs and other public sources of funding, there are several private programs that can be used to fund care and placement in guardianship cases. In this section, we will discuss some of these private programs and how they can be used to fund care and placement in Florida.

8.7.1. Insurance

Insurance is a type of private program that can be used to fund care and placement in guardianship cases. Long-term care insurance is a type of insurance policy that is designed to provide coverage for the costs associated with long-term care. This can include care in a nursing home, assisted living facility, or in-home care services. Long-term care insurance policies can provide benefits for a wide range of services, including skilled nursing care, physical therapy, and personal care services.

Long-term care insurance benefits provided by these policies can be used to pay for the costs associated with long-term care, which can be significant. In addition, long-term care insurance policies can provide flexibility in terms of the type of care and placement that is chosen. For example, if the incapacitated person would prefer to receive care in their own home rather than in a nursing home, long-term care insurance benefits can be used to pay for in-home care services.

Life insurance policies are another source of funds that can be used to fund care and placement in guardianship cases. In some cases, life insurance policies may provide a cash value that may be used to fund care. In other cases, the policy may have a provision that allows the policyholder to access some or all the death benefit early to pay for long-term care.

Life insurance can be a useful source of funding for care and placement, especially in cases where the incapacitated person has a significant life insurance policy. The death benefit provided by the policy can be used to pay for the costs associated with long-term care, such as nursing home care, assisted living facilities, or in-home care services.

An important thing to consider when applying for any type of insurance is the cost of the premiums. These insurance policies can be expensive, and the cost can vary depending on the individual's age, health status, and other factors.

8.7.2. Annuities

An annuity is a type of insurance product that provides a guaranteed income stream in exchange for a lump sum payment or a series of payments. The regular payments provided by the annuity can be used to pay for the costs associated with long-term care, such as nursing home care or in-home care services. In addition, annuities can provide a predictable source of income that can help the guardian plan for future care and placement needs.

There are two types of annuities that can be used to fund care and placement: immediate annuities and deferred annuities.

Immediate annuities provide regular payments immediately after the policyholder makes a lump sum payment, while deferred annuities provide regular payments after a certain period, typically several years. A properly structured annuity pay-out plan can allow a Medicaid applicant to protect income from the Medicaid eligibility income limits.

Immediate annuities can be a useful source of funding for care and placement. In cases where the incapacitated person requires immediate care, a lump sum payment to purchase an immediate annuity will provide regular payments that can be accessed immediately.

Deferred annuities can be a useful source of funding for care and placement in cases where the incapacitated person is not currently in need of care but may require care in the future. The policyholder can make a series of payments over a period of time, and the annuity will provide regular payments at a later date when care is needed.

8.7.3. Individual Retirement Account (IRA)

An Individual Retirement Account (IRA) is a retirement savings account that can be used as a private source of funding for care and placement in guardianship cases. If the incapacitated person has an IRA, the funds in the account can be used to pay for long-term care.

There are two types of IRAs that can be used to fund care and placement: traditional IRAs and Roth IRAs.

Traditional IRAs are funded with pre-tax contributions and withdrawals are taxed as income.

Roth IRAs are funded with after-tax contributions and withdrawals are tax-free.

One of the biggest inconveniences of using IRAs is the potential tax consequences of withdrawing funds from the account. Depending on the type of IRA, withdrawals may be subject to income tax and may also incur penalties if the policyholder is under a certain age.

Another disadvantage is the potential impact on the policyholder's retirement savings. If the policyholder withdraws funds from their IRA to pay for care and placement, they may be depleting their retirement savings and reducing the amount of funds available for their own care and living expenses in the future.

When applying for IRAs, it is recommended to work with a financial advisor or other professional who is experienced in IRAs. These professionals can help navigate the complex rules and regulations surrounding IRAs and can help identify strategies for minimizing the tax consequences of withdrawals.

8.7.4. Mutual Funds

Mutual funds can also be used to fund care and placement in guardianship cases. The funds can be used to pay for the costs associated with long-term care. In addition, mutual funds can provide a diversified investment portfolio that can help the guardian plan for future care and placement needs.

While mutual funds can be a useful source of funding, one of the biggest disadvantages to consider is the potential risk associated with investing in mutual funds. Mutual funds are subject to market fluctuations and may experience losses, which could reduce the amount of funds available to pay for care and placement.

Another problem with mutual funds is the potential impact on the policyholder's retirement savings. If the policyholder has invested a significant amount of their retirement savings in mutual funds, they may be depleting their savings and reducing the amount of funds available for their own care and living expenses in the future.

It goes without saying that it is best practice to work with a financial advisor or other professional who is experienced in mutual fund investments before making use of them. These professionals can help identify mutual funds that are designed for long-term investment and can help navigate the complex market fluctuations.

8.7.5. Bank accounts

Bank accounts can be a source of funds that can be used to pay for the costs associated with long-term care. Bank accounts can provide a convenient and easily accessible source of funds that can be used to pay for care and placement as needed.

When opening a bank account, one must pay close attention to the bank's fees and charges. Banks may charge fees for maintaining the account, making withdrawals, or transferring funds, which can reduce the amount of funds available to pay for care and placement. As such, it is best practice to compare the offerings of multiple banks and choose the one that is the most appropriate for your particular needs.

8.7.6. Assets

Assets can include a wide range of properties, such as real estate, vehicles, investments, and personal belongings, all of which can be used to fund for care and placement in guardianship cases. These assets can be sold or liquidated to generate funds that can be used to pay for long-term care.

In addition, assets can also be used to pay for the cost of legal services and other expenses associated with guardianship. For example, if the guardian needs to hire an attorney or other professional to assist with the guardianship process, they may be able to use assets to cover these costs.

One of the biggest challenges with assets is the potential cost of liquidating them. Depending on the type of asset, there may be fees associated with selling or transferring the asset, which can reduce the amount of funds available to pay for care and placement. Additionally, there may be income taxes imposed on the sale of assets.

Another challenge is the potential impact on the value of the assets. Liquidating assets can reduce the overall value of the estate, which could impact the amount of inheritance or other assets that are passed on to heirs or other beneficiaries.

8.8. Chapter Summary

This chapter has provided a comprehensive overview of the various funding sources that can be used to pay for care and placement in guardianship cases in Florida. We have covered public programs such as Medicaid and Medicare, private programs such as insurance and annuities,

8. Funding for Care and Placement

and other sources of funding such as bank accounts and assets.

One of the key takeaways from this chapter is the importance of working with professionals who are experienced in guardianship and financial planning. Attorneys, financial advisors, and other professionals can help guardians navigate the complex system of funding sources and identify strategies for protecting their loved ones' financial interests.

Another important consideration is the potential impact on the guardian's own financial security. Guardians must be careful to balance the need to provide care and placement for their loved ones with their own financial needs and obligations. This may require making difficult decisions and prioritizing financial goals.

Finally, this chapter also highlighted the importance of ongoing monitoring and evaluation of funding sources. As the situation of the incapacitated person changes, the need for funding sources may also change. Guardians must be prepared to adapt their strategies and make changes as needed.

After reading this chapter, readers should have a comprehensive understanding of the various funding sources available for care and placement in guardianship cases, and, as such, the knowledge and tools needed to navigate the system and protect their ward's and their own financial interests.

9. Managing Guardianship

9.1. Overview

In this chapter, we will delve into the key aspects of managing guardianship in Florida. As guardianship is a significant responsibility that has a profound impact on the lives of the ward and their families, understanding the different aspects of the process is essential.

But first, I will finish Lynn's story. It is a real-life case that clearly demonstrates the proper use of guardian authority and guardianship management.

Then I will return to discussing the process of obtaining or becoming a guardian in Florida, including the various steps and requirements involved. The first section of this chapter will cover topics such as the petition for incapacity, the evaluation of the alleged incapacitated person, the role of the examining committee, and the court-appointed attorney.

The next topic that will be addressed is the resignation and removal of a guardian. Guardianship is not intended to be a permanent arrangement, and there may be situations where it is necessary for a guardian to resign or be removed from their position. This section will explore the processes and legal requirements for both resigning a guardian and removing a guardian.

We will also discuss the circumstances under which a guardian may be removed, such as neglect, abuse, or mismanagement of the ward's assets.

Finally, you will learn the details of how to file a complaint in Florida. We will discuss the various channels through which a complaint can be filed, including the Florida Office of Public and Professional Guardians (OPPG), the Clerk of the Court, and the Judicial Qualifications Commission. We will also provide guidance on the documentation required and the possible outcomes of a complaint.

The importance of this chapter lies in its ability to equip you with the knowledge necessary to make informed decisions about guardianship, whether you are a potential guardian, a family member of the ward, or a professional involved in the process. By the end of this chapter, you should have a clear understanding of the various steps involved in obtaining a guardian, resigning or removing a guardian, and filing a complaint in Florida.

Case Study – Lynn's Story

A case about Loss Assets Search and Location, Medicaid Eligibility Maintenance, and Residential Placements.

Lynn's story served as a significant inspiration for this book. Among all the cases, none exhibits such a level of financial and care neglect as hers. We were appointed as the third guardian to handle her guardianship, as the previous guardians had been removed from the case due to alleged improprieties in other cases. However, Lynn's prior guardians were not removed specifically for neglecting her.

I took on the case pro bono, meaning it was a charitable endeavor. Prior to the court hearing, I met with Lynn, as I typically do with all my clients. She appeared pleasant and well-spoken. Her first comment, after brief introductions, was, "Are you going to get me out of here?"

During my initial interview, I encountered a white female, aged 65, residing in a shared room. The room was sparsely furnished and measured approximately eleven feet by fifteen feet. There was a shared bathroom that four incapacitated individuals had to utilize. Upon inspecting her closet, I discovered that she only had two pairs of clothing, one pair of shoes, and insufficiently fitting underwear. Lynn hadn't paid her room and board fees for a year, accumulating a total debt of over $37,000. During mealtimes, a two-person table was placed outside the suite doors for their meals.

Meetings with case managers and care staff appeared normal, but I pointed out that Lynn's presentation didn't exclusively indicate Alzheimer's disease. They dismissed my observation, claiming that I must have caught her on a good day.

After being appointed as Lynn's successor plenary guardian, my staff and I followed our company protocols for intake without any issues. There were no significant medical or care-related concerns initially. However, based on my preliminary observations, I instructed my staff to order new medications, as well as neurological and psychological evaluations.

In a subsequent in-person visit, Lynn reiterated that she possessed a considerable amount of money and felt trapped against her will. I raised this concern with the staff, but they dismissed her claims, stating that she often made such statements despite not having enough money to cover her fees.

Returning to Lynn's room, I asked her, "Where is your money?" To my surprise, she provided a list of banks, residential property addresses, and the names of her estranged daughter and former husband. I meticulously recorded this information. As I left her room, she called out to me, requesting a correction to her house's address, which I duly made.

Upon returning to the office, we immediately shared this information with our Case Manager of Property, instructing them to validate Lynn's claims. It turned out that she had repeatedly made these claims to guardians and center staff for over seven years, but no one had bothered to investigate them. Neither the two prior guardians, the center, nor the ward's family had taken action.

Unfortunately, this type of negligence is more common than people realize in guardianship cases involving individuals who have lost capacity, as determined by the court, and may have dementia.

Fortunately, since our office operates as a Corporate Non-Profit Guardian Company, with six capable managers on staff, we had the resources to provide a higher level of oversight and review of our cases.

Within twenty-four hours, after conducting a search of court records, we discovered a divorce settlement document related to Lynn that confirmed her claims. What had been overlooked for seven years was finally revealed.

She had been married to a business executive in a large tech firm and was a professional herself, holding a master's degree. During the divorce, they divided nearly a million dollars in family assets, with her share amounting to $492,000.

Our task was to locate the missing assets. The list of banks provided by Lynn proved to be almost 100% accurate. We swiftly located over $300,000 in cash assets, including a monthly alimony payment of $4,000, which had been consistently made as per the court order. The address of her previous home also turned out to be correct, despite the property being sold and the assets split during the divorce settlement. As of now, our search for the remaining assets is ongoing.

Before locating the missing assets, we had applied for and received Medicaid long-term care

9. Managing Guardianship

benefits and applied for Medicare rep-payee, which allowed Lynn to receive long-term medical care and assisted with the cost of the Assisted Living Facility. However, the $300,000 exceeded the Medicaid asset limit of $2,000 in Florida. To maintain her Medicaid eligibility, I petitioned the court to establish a Medicaid Pooled Trust with Aged Trust. The petition was granted, and the new assets were placed in the trust. The Pooled Trust serves as a permissible tool to safeguard assets and retain Medicaid eligibility. Funds in the trust can still be used to cover Lynn's care expenses not covered by Medicaid.

What followed was truly remarkable. Firstly, Lynn's overdue residential fees were paid in full. Then, she was relocated to a single room in a high-quality Assisted Living Facility. The room was adequately furnished, a significant improvement from her previous placement in a cramped double occupancy room with a single bed and an 18-inch shared TV. Her first request was to go shopping, and she was able to obtain a new wardrobe, hair care, and nail treatments – all reasonable requests.

Her medical evaluations continue to accurately assess her medical conditions and explore the possibility of restoring some of her rights. Lynn's short-term memory continues to defy conventional definitions of Alzheimer's disease. Her ability to recall the amount and location of her banking relationships and housing is consistently astounding. However, it was the diligent efforts of our case management system and competent staff that provided the resources necessary to deliver adequate person-centered care.

9.2. Getting a Guardian

The process of obtaining a guardian in Florida typically begins with a petition for incapacity. If the court determines that an individual is incapacitated and in need of a guardian, the judge will then appoint a guardian to oversee and manage the affairs of the incapacitated person, also known as the ward.

In this section, we will discuss the various steps involved in obtaining a guardian in Florida, as well as the different types of guardianship and the specific qualifications and requirements for each.

According to Florida Statute 744.3201, any adult may file a petition with the court to determine another person's incapacity. The petitioner must have a good faith belief that the individual in question is incapacitated and in need of a guardian. Once the petition is filed, the court will

9. Managing Guardianship

appoint an attorney to represent the interests of the alleged incapacitated person if they do not already have legal representation.

The court will appoint an examining committee of three members, usually consisting of medical and/or mental health professionals, to evaluate the alleged incapacitated person. Each member of the committee must conduct an independent examination and submit a written report detailing their findings.

The report must address the person's ability to perform essential tasks such as managing finances, making healthcare decisions, and maintaining their personal well-being. If the committee determines that the person is incapacitated, the court will hold a hearing to review the evidence and make a final decision.

The guardianship hearing allows the court to review the examining committee's reports and any other relevant evidence, including witness testimony. The alleged incapacitated person has the right to attend the hearing and may present evidence on their behalf. If the court determines that the person is incapacitated, it will then decide whether guardianship is necessary and, if so, the appropriate scope and type of guardianship to be established.

As discussed in other chapters, there are several types of guardianship in Florida, each with its specific qualifications and requirements.

A limited guardian is appointed to exercise the legal rights and powers specifically designated by the court. The court may establish a limited guardianship if it finds that the incapacitated person can perform some, but not all, of the tasks necessary to care for themselves and manage their property.

A plenary guardian is appointed to exercise all delegable legal rights and powers of the incapacitated person. This type of guardianship is established when the court determines that the person is unable to perform any of the essential tasks necessary to care for themselves and manage their property.

A professional guardian is someone who provides guardianship services to three or more wards and is not related to any of them.

Professional guardians must meet specific qualifications, including passing a Level 2 criminal background check and a credit check, completing a 40-hour training course, taking and passing a state exam, and obtaining a bond in an amount determined by the court.

9. Managing Guardianship

Once the court determines the type and scope of guardianship, it will appoint a suitable guardian.

The guardian can be a family member, friend, or professional guardian, if they meet the necessary qualifications and requirements. Florida Statute 744.312 outlines the order of preference for appointing a guardian, which generally prioritizes close relatives and individuals with a pre-existing relationship with the ward.

To serve as a guardian in Florida, an individual must be at least 18 years old, a resident of the United States, and have no felony convictions. Additionally, the individual must be capable of fulfilling the duties and responsibilities of a guardian.

Once a guardian is appointed, the court will issue Letters of Guardianship and Orders of Guardianship, which serve as legal proof of the guardian's authority to act on behalf of the ward. The scope of the guardian's powers will depend on the type of guardianship established, limited or plenary.

Guardians in Florida have various ongoing responsibilities, including managing the ward's property, making decisions about their medical care and living arrangements, and ensuring the ward's overall well-being. Guardians are required to file an annual plan with the court, which outlines the ward's medical, mental, and personal care needs, as well as an annual accounting report that details the ward's financial activities.

9.3. Resigning and Removing a Guardian

There may be situations where it is necessary for a guardian to resign or be removed from their position. In this section, we will explore the processes and legal requirements for both resigning a guardian and removing a guardian. We will also discuss the circumstances under which a guardian may be removed, such as neglect, abuse, or mismanagement of the ward's assets.

9.3.1. Resigning a Guardian

A guardian may choose to resign their position due to personal reasons, changes in circumstances, or the belief that they are no longer the best person to serve as the ward's guardian. The process for resigning as a guardian in Florida involves the following steps:

1. **Filing a Petition for Resignation:** The guardian must file a petition for resignation with the court that appointed them.

9. Managing Guardianship

This petition should include the reasons for the resignation and any relevant documentation. The court may require the guardian to provide additional information or evidence to support the request.

2. **Notice of Hearing:** The court will schedule a hearing to review the petition for resignation. All interested parties, including the ward, must be notified of the hearing date and time. This allows the interested parties to attend the hearing and present any objections or concerns.

3. **Hearing on Resignation:** During the hearing, the court will review the guardian's petition for resignation and any supporting documentation. The court may also hear testimony from the guardian, the ward, and other interested parties. If the court finds that the resignation is in the ward's best interest, it will approve the petition.

4. **Appointment of a Successor Guardian:** If the court approves the guardian's resignation, it will appoint a successor guardian to assume the responsibilities of the resigning guardian. The court will consider the ward's best interests and any

preferences expressed by the ward or other interested parties when selecting a new guardian.

5. **Final Accounting and Discharge**: The resigning guardian must submit a final accounting report detailing the ward's financial activities during the guardian's tenure. The court will review the report and, if satisfied, will discharge the guardian from their duties and responsibilities.

9.3.2. Removing A Guardian

In some cases, it may be necessary to remove a guardian due to their failure to fulfill their duties or because they are no longer suitable for the role. The process for removing a guardian in Florida is as follows:

1. **Filing a Petition for Removal:** An interested party, such as a family member, attorney, or the ward themselves, can file a petition for removal with the court that appointed the guardian. The petition should outline the reasons for the request, supported by evidence of the guardian's misconduct, neglect, or other grounds for removal.

9. Managing Guardianship

2. **Grounds for Removal:** According to Florida Statute 744.474, a guardian may be removed for various reasons, including:

   - Abuse, neglect, or exploitation of the ward.
   - Mismanagement or waste of the ward's property.
   - Failure to perform their duties or comply with court orders.
   - Conviction of a felony.
   - Development of a conflict of interest with the ward.
   - Demonstrating incapacity or poor judgment that jeopardizes the ward's best interests.

3. **Notice of Hearing:** Upon receiving the petition for removal, the court will schedule a hearing and notify all interested parties, including the ward and the guardian.

4. **Hearing on Removal**: During the hearing, the court will review the petition for removal and any supporting evidence. The court may also hear testimony from the petitioner, the guardian, the ward, and other interested parties. If the court finds sufficient grounds for removal, it will remove the guardian from their position.

Family and Professional Guardianship

5. **Appointment of a Successor Guardian:** If the court removes the guardian, it will appoint a successor guardian to assume the responsibilities of the removed guardian. The court will consider the ward's best interests and any preferences expressed by the ward or other interested parties when selecting a new guardian.

6. **Final Accounting and Discharge:** The removed guardian must submit a final accounting report detailing the ward's financial activities during their tenure. The court will review the report and, if satisfied, will discharge the removed guardian from their duties and responsibilities.

In situations where the ward is in immediate danger or at risk of suffering irreparable harm due to the guardian's actions or inactions, the court may take emergency action to protect the ward. According to Florida Statute 744.108(4), the court can appoint an emergency temporary guardian to assume the responsibilities of the current guardian until a hearing on the petition for removal can be held.

Florida law requires the court to monitor guardians to ensure they are fulfilling their duties and acting in the ward's best interests. Guardians must submit annual reports on the

9. Managing Guardianship

ward's personal well-being and financial activities, which the court reviews to identify any issues or concerns. If the court suspects misconduct, neglect, or other grounds for removal, it may initiate a removal process to protect the ward's best interests.

9.4 How to File a Complaint in Florida

In some situations, it may be necessary to file a complaint against a guardian who is not fulfilling their duties, acting inappropriately, or otherwise violating the rights of the ward. Filing a complaint ensures that the concerns are brought to the attention of the appropriate authorities and that necessary actions are taken to protect the ward's best interests. In this section, we will discuss the various channels through which a complaint can be filed in Florida, the documentation required, and the possible outcomes of a complaint.

9.4.1. Florida Office of Public and Professional Guardians (OPPG)

The Office of Public and Professional Guardians (OPPG) is a state agency responsible for monitoring—the OPPG may also refer the matter to the court for further action.

9.4.2. Clerk of the Court

If the guardian in question is not a professional guardian registered with the OPPG, you can file a complaint with the Clerk of the Court in the county where the guardianship was established. To file a complaint with the Clerk of the Court, follow these steps:

1. **Contact the Clerk's Office**: Reach out to the Clerk of the Court's office in the appropriate county and request information on how to file a complaint against a guardian. The Clerk's office will provide you with the necessary forms and instructions.

2. **Complete the Required Forms:** Fill out the complaint forms, providing detailed information about the guardian, the ward, and the nature of your complaint. Be specific and include relevant dates, locations, and any evidence to support your allegations.

3. **Submit the Forms:** Submit the completed forms and any supporting documents to the Clerk of the Court's office. The Clerk's office will review the complaint and forward it to the appropriate court division for further action.

The court will review your complaint and determine whether a hearing or investigation is warranted. If the court decides to move forward, it will notify the guardian and any other relevant parties.

If the court determines that the guardian has violated Florida's guardianship laws or failed to fulfill their duties, it may take action against the guardian, including removal or sanctions.

9.4.3. Judicial Qualifications Commission

If your complaint involves a judge's conduct in a guardianship case, you can file a complaint with the Florida Judicial Qualifications Commission (JQC). The JQC is an independent agency responsible for investigating allegations of judicial misconduct. To file a complaint with the JQC, visit the JQC website[25] for more information on how to complete and submit the complaint for.

Upon receiving your complaint, the JQC will review the information provided and determine whether an investigation is warranted. If an investigation is initiated, the JQC will contact the judge and any other relevant parties to gather additional information.

---

[25] https://floridajqc.com

If the JQC determines that the judge has violated the Florida Code of Judicial Conduct or engaged in misconduct, it may recommend disciplinary action to the Florida Supreme Court. Possible outcomes include reprimand, suspension, or removal from office.

9.4.4. Department of Children and Families (DCF) Adult Protective Services

If your complaint involves abuse, neglect, or exploitation of a vulnerable adult by a guardian, you should report it to the Department of Children and Families (DCF) Adult Protective Services. To report your concerns, follow these steps:

1. **Call the Florida Abuse Hotline**: Dial 1-800-962-2873 to report your concerns to the Florida Abuse Hotline. Trained counselors are available 24/7 to take your call.

2. **Provide Information:** Provide the counselor with detailed information about the guardian, the ward, and the nature of your complaint. Be specific and include relevant dates, locations, and any evidence to support your allegations.

If the hotline counselor determines that your complaint warrants investigation, they will forward the information to the local DCF Adult Protective Services office for further action.

In case the DCF's investigation confirms that the guardian has engaged in abuse, neglect, or exploitation, it may refer the case to law enforcement for possible criminal charges. DCF may also work with the court to ensure that appropriate actions are taken to protect the vulnerable adult.

Filling a complaint against a guardian in Florida is an essential step in ensuring that guardians are held accountable for their actions and that the rights and well-being of the ward are protected. By understanding the various channels for filing a complaint and the processes involved, you can play a crucial role in safeguarding the best interests of those under guardianship in Florida.

9.5. Chapter Summary

In this chapter, we have explored the critical aspects of managing guardianship in Florida, focusing on the processes of getting a guardian, resigning and removing a guardian, and filing a complaint.

We discussed the process of obtaining a guardian in Florida, starting with filing a petition for incapacity and moving through the stages of evaluating the alleged incapacitated person, determining the appropriate type and scope of guardianship, and appointing a suitable guardian. Understanding the many aspects of this process can help readers make informed decisions about the best course of action for themselves, a family member, or a client in need of a guardian.

We have also discussed the processes and legal requirements for resigning a guardianship and removing a guardian in Florida. We examined the circumstances under which a guardian may resign or be removed, such as neglect, abuse, or mismanagement of the ward's assets.

Understanding these procedures ensures that a guardian who is no longer suitable for the role is replaced, safeguarding the ward's well-being.

Finally, I have provided an overview of the channels through which complaints can be filed against a guardian in Florida, the documentation required, and the possible outcomes of a complaint. Filing a complaint is a vital step in holding guardians accountable for their actions and ensuring that the rights and well-being of wards are protected.

The key takeaways from this chapter on managing guardianship in Florida include understanding

9. Managing Guardianship

the process of getting a guardian, which involves filing a petition for incapacity, evaluating the alleged incapacitated person, determining the appropriate type and scope of guardianship, and appointing a suitable guardian.

I want to emphasize the importance of ongoing monitoring and oversight in the management of guardianship to guarantee that guardians continue to act in the best interests of their wards and that any issues or concerns are promptly addressed.

Managing guardianship effectively is a complex and multi-faceted endeavor that requires knowledge, vigilance, and ongoing oversight. By understanding the processes of getting a guardian, resigning and removing a guardian, and filing a complaint, as well as the importance of monitoring, education, and exploring alternatives, readers can actively participate in ensuring that individuals under guardianship receive the care, support, and protection they need

10. Conclusion and Summary

10.1 Modern Day & The Future of Guardianship

Modern-day guardianship is a complex and ever-evolving field, shaped by a variety of factors such as advancements in medical science, changes in societal attitudes towards disability and aging, and new legal developments.

In recent years, there has been increased attention paid to the potential abuse and exploitation of individuals under guardianship, leading to calls for reform and greater oversight of guardianship proceedings. This has led to changes in laws and regulations in many jurisdictions, such as increased training requirements for guardians, and the establishment of guardianship oversight boards.

One major development in modern day guardianship is the shift towards person-centered and least restrictive forms of guardianship. This approach emphasizes the autonomy and self-determination of the individual under guardianship.

Its goal is to minimize the scope of the guardian's authority and increase the individual's right to self-control and self-reliance.

This can be seen in the increased use of supported decision-making and co-guardianship models, where the individual under guardianship is supported in making their own decisions, rather than having all decision-making authority vested in a single guardian.

Additionally, the use of technology has been increasingly integrated into guardianship practices in recent years, with the use of online guardianship management systems and virtual court hearings becoming more common.

There is ongoing research and debate in the field of guardianship. Practitioners, researchers, and policymakers continue to strive for ways to effectively protect the rights and interests of individuals under guardianship, while also promoting their autonomy and wellbeing.

It is likely that future technology will play a larger role in the guardianship process. For

10. Conclusion and Summary

example, the use of remote monitoring and communication tools can enable guardians to monitor the well-being of their wards from a distance. Additionally, the use of artificial intelligence and machine learning can assist in the determination of incapacity and in the management of assets.

The trend away from institutionalization and toward community integration for individuals with disabilities will also continue to shape the future of guardianship.

This means that guardians will increasingly be responsible for helping their wards live and participate in their communities, rather than being responsible for their care in an institution.

However, the future of guardianship also brings some concerns. Some critics argue that the current guardianship system is still often overly restrictive and can lead to abuse and neglect.

They argue that alternatives such as supported decision-making, personal assistance, and other forms of self-determination must be made more widely available as an alternative to guardianship.

The need for a definitive book on guardianship in Florida has become abundantly clear to me, driven by the experiences and insights gained from handling various guardianship cases.

While a limited number of books exist on guardianship, both at a general level and specifically focused on the Florida guardianship program, they often fall short of addressing the needs of families and care professionals. Outdated resources and a dearth of readily available guidance contribute to the challenges faced by those seeking clear decision-making frameworks in selecting suitable guardians.

I have written this book to address this critical gap. By explaining the fundamental principles of guardianship and its application within the state, I hope to have provided readers with a comprehensive understanding of key topics relevant to guardianship - from the perspectives of the guardian, the ward, and the ward's family.

Each chapter of the book is meant to cover a topic that I believe is fundamental to our understanding of how guardianship works in general and in Florida in particular. Each chapter is based on information available from reputable sources and from my own experience as the founder of Hartage Foundation.

The case studies are meant to illustrate how field practice often brings challenges for which we are not trained when we become guardians

10. Conclusion and Summary

and for which precise guidelines don't exist. These studies also highlight some of the failures of the system and how it can be improved.

Let's take a closer look at how each chapter and each case study has provided useful insights and addressed some of the issues that guardians face in their profession.

In **Chapter 2**, I have provided a comprehensive overview of the history of guardianship, emphasizing its cultural, legal, and political roots and its continued relevance in modern times. As shown, throughout history, guardianship practices were an integral part of various cultures, serving to protect minors, individuals with mental disabilities, and others who were unable to care for themselves.

Roman law laid the foundation for the Western guardianship system, while English common law further shaped the modern-day guardianship system in the United States and other former British colonies.

In America, the guardianship system underwent significant changes during the colonial period and the 19th and 20th centuries, reflecting the evolving needs of society. Guardianship in Florida reflects its historical roots, with the influence of Roman law evident in its guardianship regulations.

Understanding this history provides a context for the current laws and practices, allowing us to see how the system has evolved over time and why certain aspects of the law were structured in a particular way.

Chapter 3 provides a review of the guardianship appointment process. This is a process that involves determining incapacity, filing a petition for guardianship, assessment by an examining committee, court hearings, decision-making, and finding a representing attorney.

The guardianship appointment process is not a one-time event, as the court periodically reviews the guardian's performance and may modify or terminate the guardianship if necessary. The process can be complex and time-consuming. Understanding how it works is essential for guardians, healthcare providers, and the ward's family in order to ensure that the well-being and rights of the ward are prioritized.

In **Chapter 4** I have discussed guardian compensation, a topic that might be of special interest to those who are considering becoming guardians but don't know what to expect in terms of financial compensation. Compensation for guardians can take the form of hourly or flat fee compensation, reimbursement for expenses, allowances, and miscellaneous compensation, among others.

10. Conclusion and Summary

I am sure that providers do generally care for their wards; that being said, guardian compensation is important in ensuring that the system works effectively for multiple reasons. For example, the role of a guardian can be demanding and time-consuming, and the compensation provided to a guardian can help to offset the costs of serving in this role.

A guardian is responsible for making decisions on behalf of another person who cannot make these decisions for themselves.

Chapter 5 is meant to provide a comprehensive overview of the consequences of non-compliance with reporting requirements. The chapter includes helpful information tips for completing and submitting guardianship reports and shows how to determine the reporting periods.

More specifically, this chapter highlights the importance of understanding the relationship between the Department of Elder Affairs, the Clerk of Court, and the Probate Circuit Court, as well as the requirements for the Verified Inventory Initial Report, Annual Report of the Person, and Annual Accounting of Guardian. By doing so, guardians can avoid negative legal and financial consequences.

Chapter 6 addresses the first question that needs to be answered before starting any procedure that leads to guardianship: when is it needed? The chapter discusses the criteria for determining incapacity, the guardian's family needs, issues, and processes. In addition, it provides a review of alternatives to guardianship, such as Durable Power of Attorney and Designation of Healthcare Surrogate.

As explained, while it's sometimes challenging to establish whether guardianship is needed, guardianship is often needed in cases where an individual is unable to make decisions due to a mental or physical disability. A good understanding of the procedure to establish the need for guardianship is necessary to make informed decisions that provide the necessary care and support while protecting the individual's rights and interests.

Once the need for guardianship has been established, guardians need to determine where to place the incapacitated person, a topic that is addressed in **Chapter 7**. As explained, placement options include home or community placement, independent living, assisted living facilities (ALFs), nursing homes, and skilled nursing facilities.

The placement decision can have significant consequences for the quality of life, health, and well-being of the incapacitated person. For this reason, it is strongly recommended that the cost

10. Conclusion and Summary

of the placement is at no point the only criterion used when making a decision. That being said, cost is obviously a concern, for which the chapter addresses the factors by which cost can vary.

In relation to the cost of guardianship, **Chapter 8** addresses the funding for the care and placement of the incapacitated person. There are several different sources of funding that may be available for care and placement in guardianship cases in Florida, including retirement benefits, government programs, Medicare, private programs, annuities, and mutual funds.

The chapter provides detailed information on each of these sources of funding, as well as strategies for overcoming the challenges of securing funding so that guardians can ensure that their loved ones receive the best possible care and placement while also protecting their financial interests.

Finally, in **Chapter 9** I discussed the key aspects of managing guardianship in Florida. The chapter addresses the process of obtaining a guardian, the resignation and removal of a guardian, and the process of filing a complaint in Florida.

Managing guardianship effectively is a complex issue. By understanding the processes of getting a guardian, resigning and removing a guardian, and filing a complaint, as well as the importance of monitoring, education, and exploring alternatives, one can ensure that individuals under guardianship receive the care, support, and protection they need.

There are situations where the laws & regulations outlined in these chapters don't guarantee that wards' best interests are protected. Similarly, there are situations where guardians end up handling cases for which they have not received any training.

I have two examples of such cases that have been very important in my career. First, there's **the case of Ms. Bee**, a hospitalized patient, who, as explained, was initially believed to be indigent and abandoned. However, it was later discovered that she had hidden assets. The case involved uncovering her assets, addressing her personal care needs, and finding a suitable living arrangement.

The case is an example of extortion, something which some elders who are physically or mentally impaired have experienced or are currently experiencing, without anyone but the extorters knowing. The case suggests guardians should trust their instinct and initiate an investigation when they believe it is needed. A strong suspicion is enough to do so; it is better to be proven wrong than to actually ignore such situations based on the fear of being wrong.

10. Conclusion and Summary

Lynn's story is another example of how neglect can make a ward spend years and years without access to the benefits that would otherwise be available from assets. Despite Lynn's consistent insistence that she possessed substantial assets, none of the guardians took an interest in investigating these claims.

This example should serve as an example for any guardian who has doubts about the claims made by a patient with mental impairments. Reasonable claims, even if made by a person in cognitive decline, should always be investigated.

10.2 What's Broken in Florida's Guardian System and How Can We Fix It?

Florida's guardian system plays a crucial role in safeguarding the rights and interests of individuals who are no longer capable of making their own decisions. However, there are significant shortcomings and gaps in the system that need to be addressed to ensure that wards receive the care, support, and protection they deserve.

One of the key flaws in Florida's guardian system is the inadequate investigation and verification process. This issue becomes evident when considering cases such as that of Ms. Bee, who was initially believed to be indigent and abandoned, only to later discover hidden assets. A similar situation is the case of Lynn.

Guardians must be vigilant and proactive in investigating claims and suspicions regarding a ward's financial situation. They should not solely rely on surface-level information but should diligently uncover any undisclosed assets or potential extortive situations.

However, there are no standardized guides covering such situations and many guardians simply ignore them unless the evidence is in their face.

Effective monitoring of guardians is essential to safeguarding the interests of wards. However, Florida's guardian system lacks consistent and robust monitoring mechanisms.

There is a need for systematic monitoring protocols, including regular check-ins and assessments, to evaluate the performance and conduct of guardians. Utilizing advanced technology and data systems can further enhance the monitoring process, enabling accurate tracking and identification of any red flags or concerns.

Many guardians may find themselves handling cases without having the proper training or knowledge to do so, which can lead to suboptimal outcomes for wards. To address this challenge, comprehensive training programs should be made mandatory for guardians.

These programs should cover guardianship laws, ethical responsibilities, financial management,

10. Conclusion and Summary

and other relevant topics. Collaboration with professional organizations can provide ongoing education and resources to support guardians in their roles.

Florida's guardian system should actively explore alternatives to guardianship to ensure that the least restrictive options are considered. Supported decision-making models should be promoted as an alternative to full guardianship, empowering individuals to make decisions with support from trusted individuals.

Limited guardianship should also be encouraged to preserve individual autonomy whenever appropriate. Educating families and individuals about these alternatives and providing resources for their implementation is essential.

10.3 What is the Future of Guardianship?

I believe that it will continue to be a relevant profession for many years to come. Guardianship serves as a critical mechanism to protect the well-being and rights of vulnerable individuals who are unable to make decisions for themselves due to physical or mental incapacity.

In cases where individuals face cognitive impairments such as dementia, developmental disabilities, or mental illnesses, guardianship becomes necessary to ensure their safety and well-being. It grants authority to a trusted individual or

Family and Professional Guardianship

entity to act as their legal representative, making decisions on their behalf and advocating for their rights.

Without guardianship, these individuals may be left vulnerable, with their fundamental rights compromised and their dignity at risk.

While guardianship is a vital protective measure, it is not without challenges and criticisms. Recognizing these concerns, efforts are underway to improve the guardianship system and explore alternative models that strike a balance between autonomy and protection. The future of guardianship lies in addressing these challenges and implementing reforms to enhance the efficacy, transparency, and accountability of the system.

One key aspect of reform is the need for clearer and more comprehensive legislation and regulations that govern guardianship practices. This includes defining the criteria for determining incapacity, establishing standards for guardianship training and qualifications, and creating mechanisms for ongoing oversight and monitoring.

By strengthening the legal framework, we can ensure that guardianship operates in the best interests of wards and maintains a person-centered approach.

Additionally, there is a growing recognition of the importance of less restrictive alternatives to

10. Conclusion and Summary

guardianship. Supported decision-making models empower individuals to retain their decision-making capacity with the assistance of trusted supporters.

Limited guardianship, advance directives, and power of attorney arrangements offer varying levels of decision-making authority while preserving individual autonomy. These alternatives are gaining traction as society increasingly values individual autonomy and the rights of people with disabilities.

As society continues to evolve, so too will the concept and practice of guardianship. Looking ahead, several trends and possibilities emerge, offering a glimpse into how guardianship may transform in the future.

The integration of technology into guardianship practices holds great potential for improving communication, monitoring, and decision-making. Digital platforms and applications may facilitate real-time collaboration among guardians, healthcare providers, and other stakeholders involved in the care of the ward.

Electronic health records, remote monitoring devices, and artificial intelligence systems could enhance the assessment of capacity and enable more accurate and efficient decision-making.

Family and Professional Guardianship

The future of guardianship will place a stronger emphasis on person-centered approaches, prioritizing the preferences, values, and goals of the ward. Guardians will engage in open and respectful dialogue with the ward, seeking their input and fully involving them in decision-making. This shift toward shared decision-making promotes autonomy and dignity of the ward.

This shift toward shared decision-making will promote autonomy and dignity while ensuring that the ward's best interests remain at the forefront.

GLOSSARY

Decision de Novo – translated as "anew", "from the beginning", as in an appeal of law. A court will decide the issues without reference to any legal conclusion or assumption made by the previous court.

Discovery – the process by which both parties exchange information and evidence in a court case.

Family Guardianship – appointed to a family member of the ward.

Fiduciary (Fiduciary Duty) – a person or organization that acts on behalf of another person putting their client's interests ahead of their own.

Florida Agency for Health Care Administration – the agency in Florida that administers Medicaid.

Guardian Ad Litem (GAL) – someone appointed to act in a lawsuit on behalf of a child or other person who is considered incapable of representing themselves.

Guardian Advocate – used for individuals with developmental disabilities; allows the guardian to make decisions about the ward's personal care and well-being, as well as decisions about their education and training.

Incapacity – a condition in which a person is unable to manage their property or make decisions about their own welfare due to a physical or mental impairment as determined by a court-appointed examining committee.

Limited Guardianship - used when the ward only needs assistance in specific areas of their life, such as managing their finances or making decisions about their medical care.

Nullification – invalidation; to make legally void; to cancel out.

Parens Patriae – the state regarded as legal protector of citizens who are vulnerable and/or unable to protect themselves.

Person Guardianship – used to make decisions about the ward's personal care and well-being. This includes decisions about medical treatment, living arrangements, and personal relationships.

Petitioner – someone who is seeking the appointment of a guardian for a person alleged to be incapacitated.

Plenary Guardianship – gives the guardian complete control over the ward's personal care and well-being, as well as their financial and property affairs.

Pro Bono – free of charge.

Professional Guardianship – appointed to a professional guardian who is responsible for the ward's personal care and well-being, as well as their financial and property affairs.

Property Guardianship – used to manage the ward's financial and property affairs, including decisions about assets, income, and expenses.

Spend Down - allows individuals to subtract their medical expenses from their income to bring their income below the Medicaid threshold.

Uniform Guardianship and Protective Proceedings Act (UGPPA) – outlines the rights and procedures for adults who are unable to make decisions regarding their person or property. The UGPPA provides a framework for the court to follow when determining whether guardianship is necessary and what type of guardianship is appropriate.

Veteran Guardianship – applied to veterans who are unable to make decisions about their own personal care and well-being due to a disability related to their military service.

Voluntary Guardianship - when a person voluntarily gives up the power to make decisions about their own personal care and well-being and gives it to another person.

Ward – a person who by reason of incapacity is under the protection of a court either directly or through a guardian appointed by the court.

Appendix 1

IN THE CIRCUIT COURT FOR COUNTY,
FLORIDA PROBATE DIVISION

IN RE:
File Number
Division

an alleged incapacitated person

REPORT OF EXAMINING COMMITTEE MEMBER

The undersigned, being a member of the committee appointed to examine _____ reports that such examination, as directed by the Order Appointing Examining Committee, has been completed. The report of the comprehensive examination, with evaluations and recommendations, is as follows:

Family and Professional Guardianship

I. GENERAL INFORMATION

Name of person being examined: _____
Date of birth: _____
Residence of person: _____

Date and time of examination: _____

Names of all persons present during the examination:

_____
_____
_____

If a person other than the subject of the examination answers questions posed to the alleged incapacitated person, specify the name of the person and the information provided.

Name and address of extended care facility (if any): _____

_____
_____

Alleged incapacity is: _____

DIAGNOSIS (short summary): _____

_____

Appendix 1

PROGNOSIS (short summary): _____

_____

_____

RECOMMENDED COURSE OF TREATMENT (short summary): _____

_____

_____

II. EVALUATION OF ALLEGED INCAPACITATED PERSON'S ABILITY TO RETAIN HIS OR HER RIGHTS (WITHOUT LIMITATION)

The examining committee is charged with determining whether the alleged incapacitated person has the ability to exercise those rights specified in Florida statutes section 744.3215(2) & (3) which the petitioner has requested be removed in the petition to determine incapacity.

The alleged incapacitated person has the capacity to: (Choose yes or no)

YES	NO	Make and exercise informed decisions regarding his/her right to marry.
YES	NO	Make and exercise informed decisions regarding his/her right to vote.

Family and Professional Guardianship

YES	NO	Make and exercise informed decisions regarding his/her right to personally apply for government benefits.
YES	NO	Make and exercise informed decisions regarding his/her right to have a driver's license and operate a motor vehicle.
YES	NO	Make and exercise informed decisions regarding his/her right to travel.
YES	NO	Make and exercise informed decisions regarding his/her right to seek or retain employment.
YES	NO	Make and exercise informed decisions regarding his/her right to contract.
YES	NO	Make and exercise informed decisions regarding his/her right to sue, or assist in the defense of suits of any nature against him or her.
YES	NO	Make informed decisions regarding and exercise his/her right to manage property or to make any gift or disposition of property.
YES	NO	Make and exercise informed decisions determining his/her residence.
YES	NO	Make and exercise informed decisions regarding his/her right to consent to medical and mental health treatment.

| YES | NO | Make informed decisions affecting the social environment or other social aspects of his/her life. |

III. COMPREHENSIVE EXAMINATION

Please give the results of the comprehensive examination and the committee member's assessment of information provided by the attending or family physician, if any. Attach extra sheets if necessary. If the attending or family physician is available for consultation, the committee member must consult with the physician.

Physical Examination: _____

_____

Mental Health Examination: _____

_____

Functional Assessment: _____

_____

If any of the three parts of the comprehensive examination were not indicated or could not be accomplished for any reason, the reason for the omission must be explained.

Consultation with Family Physician:
Yes ☐ No ☐ If no, why? _____

Assessment of information provided by attending or family physician, if any:

_____
_____
_____

Assessment of prior clinical history, treatment records, social records, and reports, if any:

_____
_____
_____

Please list specific evidence of the person's incapacity to exercise informed decisions in the categories previously checked:

_____
_____

IV. SCOPE OF GUARDIANSHIP (IF ANY)

If the examiner has determined that the alleged incapacitated person is incapacitated and if the court finds guardianship to be necessary, the scope of the guardianship recommended is:

PLENARY LIMITED (Choose one)

I certify that I have examined the alleged incapacitated person in accordance with the requirements of Section 744.331, Florida Statutes, performing the examination necessary to determine which, if any, of the rights the petitioner has requested to be removed the allegedly incapacitated person can no longer sufficiently nor adequately exercise. These conclusions, evaluations and recommendations are hereby presented to the Court.

I have knowledge of the type of incapacity alleged in the Petition to Determine Incapacity. Executed this day of _____

Signature: _____

Typed or printed name: _____

A copy of this report has been served on the petitioner's attorney and the court appointed attorney for the alleged incapacitated person by _____ on _____.

[Print or Type Names Under All Signature Lines]

Bar Form No. G-2.051 - 4 of 4

Appendix 2

MODEL FORM FOR USE IN PETITION
TO DETERMINE
INCAPACITY PURSUANT TO FLORIDA
PROBATE RULE 5.550

In the Circuit Court of the
Judicial Circuit,
in and for (County), Florida

Probate Division
Case No. _____

In Re: Guardianship of _____
Respondent's Name
An Alleged Incapacitated Person

PETITION TO DETERMINE INCAPACITY

Petitioner, _____(name of petitioner), files this petition seeking a determination of incapacity of the respondent and states:

1. Petitioner's name: _____

2. Petitioner's age: _____

3. Petitioner's home address: _____
_____

4. Petitioner's mailing address: _____
_____

5. Petitioner's relationship to the respondent: _
_____
_____

6. Respondent's name: _____

7. Respondent's age: _____

8. Respondent's home address: _____
_____

9. Respondent's mailing address: _____
_____

Appendix 2

10. Respondent's county of residence:_____
_____

11. Respondent's primary language:_____

12. The factual basis for alleging incapacity:___
_____
_____

13. List all persons with their name and address known to have information relating to the basis for alleging incapacity.

a. Name_____
Address_____
City_____State_____Zip_____

b. Name_____
Address_____
City_____State_____Zip_____

c. Name_____
Address_____
City_____State_____Zip_____

14. Which rights are being sought to be removed under section 744.3215, Florida Statutes? Indicate which rights that the petitioner requests be removed from the respondent, but not delegated to a guardian:

☐ a. To marry. (If the right to enter into a contract has been removed, the right to marry is subject to court approval.)

☐ b. To vote.

☐ c. To personally apply for government benefits.

☐ d. To have a driver license.

☐ e. To travel.

☐ f. To seek or retain employment.

Indicate which rights that the petitioner requests be removed from the respondent, but may be delegated to the guardian:

☐ a. To contract;

☐ b. To sue and defend lawsuits;

☐ c. To apply for government benefits;

☐ d. To manage property or to make any gift or disposition of property;

☐ e. To determine his or her residence;

☐ f. To consent to medical and mental health treatment; and

☐ g. To make decisions about his or her social environment or other social aspects of his or her life.

If all of the above are checked, a determination of plenary incapacity is requested. If only some of the above are checked a determination of limited incapacity is requested.

15. Is a guardianship being sought?
Yes ☐ No ☐

Check any possible alternatives to guardianship:

☐ a. Trust agreements;

☐ b. Powers of attorney;

☐ c. Designations of health care surrogates;

☐ d. Other advance directives; or

☐ e. Other

If a guardianship is being sought, explain why the checked possible alternatives to guardianship are insufficient to meet the needs of the respondent:

_____
_____
_____

16. List the names, addresses, phone numbers, and relationships of the living next of kin of the respondent, including date of birth if the person is a minor. If married, this includes the spouse and all of his or her children:

Appendix 2

Name of the Living Next of Kin of the Respondent

Name:_____
Address: _____
City:_____ State_____ Zip_____
Phone Cell:_____ Landline: _____
Date of birth if person is a minor: _____

Name:_____
Address: _____
City:_____ State_____ Zip_____
Phone Cell:_____ Landline: _____
Date of birth if person is a minor: _____

Name:_____
Address: _____
City:_____ State_____ Zip_____
Phone Cell:_____ Landline: _____
Date of birth if person is a minor: _____

WHEREFORE, this court is respectfully requested to determine incapacity of the respondent, award attorney's fees and costs pursuant to Chapter 744, Florida Statutes, and grant such other relief as the court deems just and proper.

Under penalties of perjury, I declare that I have read the foregoing, and the facts alleged are true, to the best of my knowledge and belief.

Signed: _____

Date: _____

Petitioner's Signature _____

Petitioner's Printed Name: _____

Petitioner's Address: _____

_____

Petitioner's Phone Number:_____

Petitioner's E-mail Address: _____

Bibliographies
By Chapter

Chapter 1

Bell, W. G., et al. (1981). "Public guardianship and the elderly: Findings from a national study." *The Gerontologist* **21**(2): 194-202.

Campbell, K. P., et al. (2016). "The restoration of capacity for persons under guardianship with developmental disabilities in Florida." J. Int'l Aging L. & Pol'y **9**: 55.

Commission, U. L. (1997). Uniform guardianship and protective proceedings act.

Courts, F. "Guardianship." Retrieved 01/30, 2023, from https://www.flcourts.gov/Resources-Services/Office-of-Family-Courts/Family-Courts/Guardianship.

David, M. S. (2011). "Legal guardianship of individuals incapacitated by mental illness: where do we draw the line." Suffolk UL Rev. **45**: 465.

Diller, R. (2016). "Legal capacity for all: Including older persons in the shift from adult guardianship to supported decision-making." Fordham Urb. LJ **43**: 495.

Schmidt, W. C., et al. (2017). "Program and ward characteristics and cost savings of public guardianship: an evaluation of the Florida public guardianship program." U. Fla. JL & Pub. Pol'y **28**: 329.

Teaster, P. B., et al. (2007). "Wards of the state: A national study of public guardianship." Stetson L. Rev. **37**: 193.

Wright, J. L. (2010). "Guardianship for your own good: Improving the well-being of respondents and wards in the USA." International journal of law and psychiatry **33**(5-6): 350-368.

Chapter 2

Aikin, B. F. (2016). "Why the Fiduciary Standard Exists." Journal Of Financial Planning **29**(8): 17-19.

Blackstone, W. (1765). Sir, Commentaries on the Laws of England, Vol. II. para 1, 4 vols, Oxford University Press.

Coleman, D. and T. Nerney "Guardianship and the Disability Rights Movement."

Constitution, F. (1868). "Constitution of the State of Florida." Adopted February **25**: 1868.

Cook, T. M. (1991). "The americans with disabilities act: The move to integration." Temp. LR **64**: 393.

Dix, D. (2015). "R eformer and activist Dorothea Lynde Dix was one of the most prominent advocates for the mentally ill in American history. Her tireless lobbying of government officials led to dramatic reforms in mental health care, as well as to the creation of the nation's first mental asylums. In her long and successful career, Dix also helped found schools for the mentally handicapped." The Early Republic and Antebellum America: An Encyclopedia of Social, Political, Cultural, and Economic History: 299.

Gladstone, D. (2002). The Changing Dynamic of Institutional Care: The Western Counties Idiot Asylum 1864–1914 1. From idiocy to mental deficiency, Routledge: 134-160.

Grossberg, M. (1983). "Who gets the child? Custody, guardianship, and the rise of a judicial patriarchy in nineteenth-century America." Feminist Studies **9**(2): 235-260.

Heffner, M. B. (2016). "From Idiots and Lunatics to Incapacitated Persons and Respondents: The Evolution of Guardianship Law in Rhode Island." Roger Williams UL Rev. **21**: 554.

Helmholz, R. H. (1977). "Roman Law of Guardianship in England, 1300-1600." Tul. L. Rev. **52**: 223.

Hubert, H. L. (1994). "In the Child's Best Interests: The Role of the Guardian Ad Litem in Termination of Parental Rights Proceedings." U. Miami L. Rev. **49**: 531.

Laidlaw, K., et al. (2010). "Attitudes to ageing and expectations for filial piety across Chinese and British cultures: A pilot exploratory evaluation." Aging & Mental Health **14**(3): 283-292.

Lewis, J. J. D. "100th Anniversary of the Juvenile Court 1899–1999."

Miller, T. L. and H. N. Switzky (1978). "The least restrictive alternative: Implications for service providers." The Journal of Special Education **12**(2): 123-131.

Morgan, R. C. (2013). <u>Least Restrictive Alternative, Limited Guardianship and the Ward's Autonomy. Trends in the United States in the 21st Century</u>. Adult Guardianship Law for the 21st Century, Nomos Verlagsgesellschaft mbH & Co. KG.

Ratliff, J. (1999). "Parens patriae: An overview." <u>Tul. L. Rev.</u> **74**: 1847.

Rowse, T. (2014). "Population knowledge and the practice of guardianship." <u>American Nineteenth Century History</u> **15**(1): 15-42.

Schriner, K. and L. A. Ochs (2001). "Creating the disabled citizen: How Massachusetts disenfranchised people under guardianship." <u>Ohio St. LJ</u> **62**: 481.

Sherman, C. P. (1913). "Debt of the Modern Law of Guardianship to Roman Law." <u>Mich. L. Rev.</u> **12**: 124.

St. Jean, W. B. (1999). "Inventing Guardianship: The Mohegan Indians and Their" Protectors"." <u>The New England Quarterly</u> **72**(3): 362-387.

Teitelbaum, L. E. (1985). "Family history and family law." <u>Wis. L. Rev.</u>: 1135.

Venter, E. (2004). "The notion of ubuntu and communalism in African educational discourse." <u>Studies in philosophy and education</u> **23**: 149-160.

Walker, S. S. (1984). "Common Law Juries and Feudal Marriage Customs in Medieval England: The Pleas of Ravishment." <u>U. Ill. L. Rev.</u>: 705.

Witte Jr, J. and F. S. Alexander (2007). <u>The teachings of modern Roman Catholicism on law, politics, and human nature</u>, Columbia University Press.

Chapter 3

Courts, F. "Guardianship." Retrieved 01/30, 2023, from https://www.flcourts.gov/Resources-Services/Office-of-Family-Courts/Family-Courts/Guardianship.

Guardian, R. O. and G. A. Litem "Florida Probate Rules."

Kelly, A. M., et al. (2021). "A 50-state review of guardianship laws: Specific concerns for special needs planning." <u>J Financ Serv Prof</u> 75(1).

Statutes, F. (2021). "Chapter 744.331, Proceedings to review capacity determination." Retrieved 02/13, 2023, from https://www.flsenate.gov/Laws/Statutes/2021/Chapter744/All.

Statutes, T. F. (2022). "744.108 Guardian and attorney fees and expenses." Retrieved 02/13, 2023, from http://www.leg.state.fl.us/Statutes/index.cfm?App_mode=Display_Statute&Search_String=&URL=0700-0799/0744/Sections/0744.108.html.

Sun, T., et al. (2020). "Decision-making under ambiguity or risk in individuals with Alzheimer's disease and mild cognitive impairment." Frontiers in psychiatry 11: 218.

Chapter 4

A. T. F. S. i. S. S. (2022). "744.2001 Office of Public and Professional Guardians." Retrieved 02/27, 2023, from http://www.leg.state.fl.us/statutes/index.cfm?mode=View%20Statutes&SubMenu=1&App_mode=Display_Statute&Search_String=Statewide+Public+Guardianship+Office&URL=0700-0799/0744/Sections/0744.2001.html.

Casetext.com. "Jones v. Jones." from https://casetext.com/case/jones-v-jones-62568.

Martin, L. (2003). "Making performance-based contracting perform: What the federal government can learn from the state and local governments." The Procurement Revolution, Rowman & Littlefield, New York: 87-125.

Statutes, F. (2021). "Chapter 744.108, Compensation of guardians." Retrieved 02/13, 2023, from https://www.flsenate.gov/Laws/Statutes/2021/Chapter744/All.

ZipRecruiter (2023). "How much does a Gurdianship make in Florida?". Retrieved 02/26, 2023, from https://www.ziprecruiter.com/Salaries/Guardianship-Salary--in-Florida#:~:text=How%20much%20does%20a%20Guardianship,%2Fweek%20or%20%243%2C729%2Fmonth.

Chapter 5

Karp, N. and E. F. Wood (2007). "Guardianship monitoring: A national survey of court practices." Stetson L. Rev. 37: 143.

Statues, F. (2023). "The 2022 Florida Statutes (including 2022 Special Session A and 2023 Special Session B)." Retrieved 03/07, 2023, from http://www.leg.state.fl.us/statutes/index.cfm?App_mode=Display_Statute&URL=0400-0499/0430/0430ContentsIndex.html.

Statutes, F. (2023). "Title XLIII, Chapter 744, Section 744.362." Retrieved 03/07, 2023, from http://www.leg.state.fl.us/statutes/index.cfm?mode=View%20Statutes&SubMenu=1&App_mode=Display_Statute&Search_String=Verified+Inventory+Initial+Report&URL=0700-0799/0744/Sections/0744.362.html.

Statutes, F. (2023). "Title XLIII, Chapter 744, Section 744.3021." Retrieved 03/07, 2023, from http://www.leg.state.fl.us/statutes/index.cfm?App_mode=Display_Statute&URL=0700-0799/0744/Sections/0744.3021.html.

Statutes, F. (2023). "Title XLIII, Chapter 744, Section 744.3021 744.331." Retrieved 03/07, 2023, from http://www.leg.state.fl.us/statutes/index.cfm?App_mode=Display_Statute&Search_String=&URL=0700-0799/0744/Sections/0744.331.html.

Statutes, F. (2023). "Title XLIII, Chapter 744, Section 744.3675." Retrieved 03/07, 2023, from http://www.leg.state.fl.us/statutes/index.cfm?mode=View%20Statutes&SubMenu=1&App_mode=Display_Statute&Search_String=744.3675&URL=0700-0799/0744/Sections/0744.3675.html.

Uekert, B. K. and R. Schauffler (2009). "The need for improved adult guardianship data." Judicature 93: 201.

Chapter 6

Alcohol, D. A. (1989). "Mental Health Program Office: Annual report to the Florida Legislature." Florida Department of Health and Rehabilitative Services.

Desai, A. and A. O. Giwa (2019). "Power of Attorney."

Families, F. D. o. C. a. "Baker Act." Retrieved 21/03, 2023, from https://www.myflfamilies.com/crisis-services/baker-act.

Lemieux, A. E. (2020). "The Baker Act: Time for Florida to get its act together." Child & Fam. LJ 8: 117.

LHRM, C. (2008). "Baker Act Basics."

Oaks, D. H. (1966). "Legal History in the High Court: Habeas Corpus." Michigan Law Review 64(3): 451-472.

Statutes, F. (2023). "Florida Statutes, Chapter CCCXCVII". Retrieved 03/07, 2023, from http://www.leg.state.fl.us/statutes/index.cfm?App_mode=Display_Statute&Search_String=&URL=0700-0799/0744/Sections/0744.331.html.

Statutes, F. (2023). "Florida Statutes, Chapter DCCXLIV, Section 744.102(12)". Retrieved 03/07, 2023, from http://www.leg.state.fl.us/statutes/index.cfm?App_mode=Display_Statute&Search_String=&URL=0700-0799/0744/Sections/0744.331.html.

Statutes, F. (2023). "Florida Statutes, Chapter VII IX". Retrieved 03/07, 2023, from http://www.leg.state.fl.us/statutes/index.cfm?App_mode=Display_Statute&Search_String=&URL=0700-0799/0744/Sections/0744.331.html.

Statutes, F. (2023). "Florida Statutes, Chapter CCCXCIV, Section 394.451." Retrieved 03/07, 2023, from http://www.leg.state.fl.us/statutes/index.cfm?App_mode=Display_Statute&Search_String=&URL=0700-0799/0744/Sections/0744.331.html.

Statutes, F. (2023). "Florida Statutes, Chapter DC LXV". Retrieved 03/07, 2023, from http://www.leg.state.fl.us/statutes/index.cfm?App_mode=Display_Statute&Search_String=&URL=0700-0799/0744/Sections/0744.331.html.

Sweeney, T. J., et al. (2013). "Civil commitment for substance use disorder patients under the Florida Marchman Act: demographics and outcomes in the private clinical setting." Journal of addictive diseases 32(1): 108-115.

Chapter 7

Alvarez, J. A. (2019). "Florida Needs to Protect Grandma & Grandpa.". Thomas L. Rev. **32**: 31.

Ball, M. M., et al. (2004). "Independence in assisted living." Journal of Aging Studies **18**(4): 467-483.

Genworth (2021). "Cost of Care Survey." Retrieved 07/27, 2023, from https://www.genworth.com/aging-and-you/finances/cost-of-care.html.

Gonzalez, L. (2022). "Long-term care options in Florida: Their availability by county demographics." Journal of Racial and Ethnic Health Disparities **9**(2): 698-707.

Metcalf, C. A. (1986). "A response to the problem of elder abuse: Florida's revised adult protective services act." Fla. St. UL Rev. **14**: 745.

Sousa, L. and D. Figueiredo (2002). "Dependence and independence among old persons–realities and myths." Reviews in Clinical Gerontology **12**(3): 269-273.

Weissert, W. G., et al. (1988). "The past and future of home-and community-based long-term care." The Milbank Quarterly: 309-388.

Chapter 8

Aging, A. C. o. (2023). "Florida Medicaid Eligibility: 2023 Income & Assets Limits." Retrieved 04/03, 2023, from https://www.medicaidplanningassistance.org/medicaid-eligibility-florida/.

Burkhauser, R. V. and M. Daly (2011). The declining work and welfare of people with disabilities: What went wrong and a strategy for change, AEI Press.

Feinberg, L., et al. (2011). "Valuing the invaluable: 2011 update, the growing contributions and costs of family caregiving." Washington, DC: AARP Public Policy Institute **32**: 2011.

Fichtner, J. J. and J. S. Seligman (2018). "Saving Social Security Disability Insurance: Designing and Testing Reforms through Demonstration Projects." Mercatus Research Paper.

Goss, S. C. (2010). "The future financial status of the social security program." Soc. Sec. Bull. **70**: 111.

Ibbotson, R. G. (2010). "The importance of asset allocation." Financial Analysts Journal **66**(2): 18-20.

Kubik, J. D. (1999). "Incentives for the identification and treatment of children with disabilities: the supplemental security income program." Journal of Public Economics **73**(2): 187-215.

Maurer, R. and W. Horneff (2007). "The Calculus of Retirement Income: Financial Models for Pension Annuities and Life Insurance. By Moshe A. Milevsky. Cambridge University Press, 2006, ISBN 0-521-84258-1, 321 pages, Price $45.00." Journal of Pension Economics & Finance **6**(1): 102-104.

Pesner, M. (2021). "Public Pensions and Retirement: Evidence from the Railroad Retirement Act." Manuscript, Vanderbilt University.

Poterba, J. M. (2014). "Retirement security in an aging population." <u>American Economic Review</u> **104**(5): 1-30.

Servon, L. (2017). <u>The unbanking of America: How the new middle class survives</u>, Houghton Mifflin Harcourt.

Shadowen, H. and A. J. Barnes (2022). "Medicaid can and should play an active role in advancing health equity."

Sialm, C. (2009). "Tax changes and asset pricing." <u>American Economic Review</u> **99**(4): 1356-1383.

Slott, E. (2012). <u>The Retirement Savings Time Bomb... and How to Defuse It: A Five-Step Action Plan for Protecting Your IRAs, 401 (k) s, and Other Retirement Plans from Near Annihilation by the Taxman</u>, Penguin.

Weaver, D. A. (2001). "The widow (er)'s limit provision of Social Security." <u>Soc. Sec. Bull.</u> **64**: 1.

Zweig, J. (2015). <u>The Devil's Financial Dictionary</u>, PublicAffairs.

Chapter 9

Fell, N. (1994). "Guardianship and the Elderly Oversight Not Overlooked." <u>U. Tol. L. Rev.</u> **25**: 189.

Frolik, L. A. (1998). "Guardianship reform: When the best is the enemy of the good." Stan. L. & Pol'y Rev. **9**: 347.

Hurme, S. B. and E. Wood (2001). "Guardian accountability then and now: Tracing tenets for an active court role." Stetson L. Rev. **31**: 867.

Statutes, F. (2023). "Florida Statutes, Chapter DCCXLIV". Retrieved 04/03, 2023, from http://www.leg.state.fl.us/statutes/index.cfm?mode=View%20Statutes&SubMenu=1&App_mode=Display_Statute&Search_String=744.312&URL=0700-0799/0744/Sections/0744.312.html.

Printed in the USA
CPSIA information can be obtained
at www.ICGtesting.com
LVHW071712030424
776321LV00013B/257